GLEANINGS
IN
AFRICA;

EXHIBITING

A FAITHFUL AND CORRECT VIEW

OF THE

MANNERS AND CUSTOMS OF THE INHABITANTS

OF THE

CAPE OF GOOD HOPE,

AND SURROUNDING COUNTRY.

With a full and comprehensive Account of the System of Agriculture adopted
by the Colonists:

*Soil, Climate, Natural Productions,
&c. &c. &c.*

INTERSPERSED WITH OBSERVATIONS AND REFLECTIONS

ON THE

State of Slavery

In the Southern Extremity of

THE AFRICAN CONTINENT.

In a Series of Letters from an English Officer during the Period in which that
Colony was under the Protection of

THE BRITISH GOVERNMENT.

ILLUSTRATED WITH ENGRAVINGS.

NEGRO UNIVERSITIES PRESS
NEW YORK

Originally published in 1806
by James Cundee, Ivy-Lane, London

Reprinted 1969 by
Negro Universities Press
A DIVISION OF GREENWOOD PUBLISHING CORP.
NEW YORK

SBN 8371-1133-1

PRINTED IN UNITED STATES OF AMERICA

THE

EDITOR'S PREFACE.

THE small collection of Letters here presented to the public, was not originally intended for any such purpose, and would never have gone abroad, had not several persons of distinguished taste and abilities, as well as of extensive information, solicited the publication, being convinced that it would exhibit a fund of valuable instruction and rational amusement. In this respect, indeed, it is presumed that the reader will not be disappointed, but will find a great deal both of the useful and the agreeable comprised within a narrow compass.

The following sheets consist of a Series of Letters from a gentleman who resided a considerable time at the Cape of Good Hope, during the period in which that celebrated Dutch settlement so much talked of, and so little known in this country, was in the possession of the British government. The letters are interesting, sentimental, and strikingly descriptive both of men, manners, and the scenery of Nature in that part

*part of the world. He appears to have been a
person of accurate observation and refined sentiments. He possessed the most ample means of
acquiring a knowledge of the manners and customs of the colonists, as well as of the agricultural system in use among them, and examined,
with the eye of a philosopher, the whole œconomy
of the settlement. His description of the face
of the country, and the situations of the principal villages, farms, and plantations dispersed in
various parts of the colony, are singularly animated and picturesque ; and his observations on
the habits of life among the colonists, are judicious and interesting : and, upon the whole, the
information which we find contained in these
Letters, although concentrated within a narrow
compass, is, perhaps, as accurate and extensive
as any that has ever been obtained in this country relative to the southern extremity of the
African continent. The sensibility of his heart
corresponds with the acuteness of his observation, and we cannot read his remarks and reflections on slavery, without experiencing in our
breasts, a sympathetic unison with his feelings.*

*The Letters are written in the plain and un-
studied style of familiar correspondence, the un-
affected but expressive language of one friend
speaking*

*speaking to another, which renders them not less,
but more valuable.   While we read the Letters,
we seem indeed to be conversing with the writer,
and accompanying the traveller in his excursions,
to join in his remarks, and participate in his
reflections and sentiments; and while we must
acknowledge that he is perfectly qualified to observe, reflect and compare, we cannot but perceive, at the same time, that to those talents so
essential to a traveller, he unites the inestimable
virtues of attachment to the constitution of his
country, and loyalty to his Sovereign.*

*In a well-grounded confidence that the expecta-
tion of the public will not be disappointed in this
small performance, it is laid before the reader*

By his very humble servant,

THE EDITOR.

CONTENTS.

LETTER III.

LETTER IV.

LETTER V.

LETTER

CONTENTS.

LETTER

LETTER XV.

LETTER XVI.

LETTER XVII.

LETTER XXIV.

LETTER XXV.

LETTER XXVI.

LETTER XXVII.

LETTER

LETTER XXXIV.

LETTER XXXV.

LETTER XXXVI.

LETTER XXXVII.

LETTER XXXVIII.

LETTER XXXIX.

GLEANINGS

IN

AFRICA.

LETTER I.

Departure from England---Proceed under the convoy of a fri-
gate---Dark and hazy weather---The tempestuous gales of the
Bay of Biscay fortunately escaped---Porto Zanto---Remarks on
the island of Madeira and the north-east trade wind---The
tropic of Cancer crossed---Flying fishes---A singular circumstance of a swallow---Calms and variable weather prevalent
in low latitudes---Description of a storm---The equator crossed
---Ceremonies among the sailors peculiar to the occasion---
Remarks on the south-east trade-wind---A look-out for the
land of Africa---Good water an essential article at sea---Chi-
nese mode of purifying it---The Lascar sailors harshly treated
---Their dulness in cold, and activity in warm climates.

To my dear friend I cheerfully impart
the various observations which I have made
since my departure from old England, and,
though you may have read many histories
of the country whereof I shall treat, yet, as
the remarks of mankind vary according to
their

their several dispositions, I flatter myself that these my communications will contain a sufficient portion of interesting, as well as original information, to claim your attention; at all events they have one strong recommendation, and that is, a strict adherence to *truth*, for it is not the part of real friendship (such as I profess) to deceive.

On the 17th of March we having got under weigh, favored with a light breeze from the north-east, the shores of dear England gradually receded from us. The novelty of the surrounding scene, added to the bustle and confusion which attended our departure, for a moment suppressed the rising sigh, and rendered less poignant those sensations, which a separation from our country, friends, and all that is dear, naturally excites.

We proceeded under convoy of a frigate, that kept at bay those sneaking privateers which infest the channel. The weather was so dark and hazy, that as we went along we could hardly discern the English coast. On the third day (March 20) we found

found ourselves clear of the British channel, and having entered the stormy Atlantic, were skirting along the Bay of Biscay, where ships generally meet with tempestuous gales; we were, however, fortunate in having escaped them. The weather still continued cold and cloudy, but the hope of soon feeling the enlivening influence of a southern climate, banished all gloomy sensations.

The more we advanced the less we were annoyed with the rolling of the vessel; —many of the passengers were fortunate enough to escape sea-sickness, while those who suffered became the objects of their sport. Custom reconciles us to these scenes, —what a novice might think a violent gale, the hardy son of Neptune would regard only as a gentle breeze.

On the morning of the 31st we came in sight of Porto Zanto, one of the Madeira islands. Under an easy press of sail, we found ourselves towards evening coasting along the island of Madeira, which is more generally known by that name.

Towards

Towards the middle, this island assumes
an elevated appearance; and from the point
of view we beheld it, by no means corresponds with those ideas of fertility which
are entertained of it. A brisk gale from the
north-east drove us rapidly along, and night
approaching, its aspiring cliffs, and every
other object, were enveloped in surrounding
darkness.

We had now fairly entered the north-east
trade-wind. The degree of north latitude
that this wind is to be met with, is in some
degree regulated by the season of the year,
and the sun's distance north or south of the
equator.—On the morning of the 4th of April
we crossed the tropic of Cancer, and the
weather became remarkably warm; but the
cool, refreshing breeze that here invariably
blows, gives a bracing temperature to the
air, and renders confinement less irksome.

When about the latitude of 13º north, we
for the first time perceived numbers of flying
fish in every direction. At first sight they
might naturally be mistaken for small birds
skimming along the surface of the ocean:
their flight, though rapid, cannot be long
continued,

continued, from the smallness of their fins. Even in this silent and solitary region of trackless ocean, these little sportive fish are not without their enemies; the larger fish prey upon them; and when, to escape impending danger, they betake themselves to flight, they are eagerly pursued by a variety of sea-birds. It is no unamusing spectacle, I assure you, to observe their dexterity in the pursuit;—thus, to avoid *Scylla,* they unfortunately strike upon *Charybdis.*

I must not here omit mentioning a circumstance which to me, indeed, appeared somewhat singular. Being in about 9° 30′ north latitude, and the African coast more than three hundred miles distant, I was agreeably surprised by the appearance of a swallow that crossed and re-crossed the ship several times, without venturing to alight on any part of the rigging. Whence had it come? whither was it going? or, had it sustained so long a flight from land as our present distance from it? These were questions which naturally occurred, and a diversity of conjectures consequently employed my mind. At one time I imagined it had accompanied

companied us in our passage from England,
—that it might hitherto have been in a tor-
pid state, concealed in some corner or cre-
vice of the ship, and on feeling the genial
warmth of our approach to the line, might
have become re-animated. I should hardly
have supposed that this poor solitary bird
ventured across the deep unattended by any
of its species. Such, however, was the case,
and I shall leave my friend to form his own
conjectures.

On a near approach to the equator, the
north-east trade-wind gradually dies away,
and we then begin to meet with those calms
so frequently experienced by navigators in
crossing this grand line of demarkation between the northern and the southern he-
mispheres of the world. Add to these the
tainted atmosphere of a crowded ship, where
disease and death already made great havock, though the better half of our voyage
was still before us. Amidst this darkening
prospect, I felt quite resigned to my fate,
and committed myself to the protection of
that power who sees through all futurity,
and whose omnipotence and wisdom are
demonstrated

demonstrated by his mercies. Here, my friend, an eternal summer reigns. In vain we endeavoured to relieve the eye from the dull uniformity of the surrounding scene,—in vain we looked for the verdant meadow, or the flowery field: the heavens above, and the boundless ocean, day after day, alone presented themselves to our view. No longer we enjoyed the serene sky that accompanied us on running down the north-east trade-winds. Calms and variable weather alike prevail in these low latitudes. The forked lightning illuminated the whole horizon; the roaring thunder assailed the ear, and the violent torrents threatened destruction! In vain my feeble pen attempts to give a descriptive coloring to this truly awful scene! Picture it to yourself, my friend, and let imagination conceive what no tongue can express:—the night dark, but irradiated at intervals with vivid flashes of lightning; —the reiterated peals of thunder, rending, as it were, the heavens;—and quick in succession the descending torrents, that almost drowned even Neptune's sons. We hailed returning day with gratitude! we rejoiced

in

in having survived the storm. It seems, my friend, we had directed our course too far to the east, where ships are more liable to be becalmed. On the 30th we crossed the equator, and congratulated each other on entering the southern hemisphere. Among the sailors it was a day of merriment and festivity. It is customary, on crossing the equator, to initiate young sailors into the mysteries of their profession, by the performance of some ridiculous ceremonies peculiar to the occasion. Neptune, Amphitrite, Triton, and all the sea-born family make their appearance. They hail the ship, and are invited to come on board. They inquire whence comes the vessel? and whither bound? I own I am much entertained with the company of those who for the first time have visited the southern world. Such are paraded before the marine deity, who assumes a profound air of dignity and authority on the occasion. We all answered his commands in our turn. With some he would not depart from the mysterious rites of initiation; to others he was more lenient, excusing them altogether of submitting to the operation

operation of what sailors term *shaving*. From their intercourse with Europeans, Neptune and his attendants were taught to expect a portion of brandy, and having received the customary tribute, they departed to their respective stations.

The south-east trade-wind having come to our relief, the face of the heavens was again mild and serene. This wind is by no means so steady as that of the northern hemisphere, at least we did not find it so, for it varied continually, and was sometimes as high as east north-east.

It has been remarked, that beyond the parallel of 16° south latitude, the south-east trade-wind has been found to incline to the north; but this is in some measure influenced by the season of the year, and the sun's greater or less distance from the northern tropic; and may in like manner be found to hang to the south, on the sun's return to the southern tropic.

You are probably, by this time, as anxious to get to the conclusion of this letter, as I was to the end of my voyage, therefore I shall spare you the dull monotonous detail

of

of the remaining part; suffice it to say, that we have just approached that point in our reckoning which promises in a few hours to show us the projecting land of Africa; and now, while all on deck are keeping a good look out, allow me to close this epistle with a few remarks, that have forcibly obtruded themselves on my mind.

During a long voyage we necessarily learn the value of a number of articles, which, when on shore, we totally disregard, or do not sufficiently estimate. Here we must have every thing within ourselves; our stores previously provided, our foresight exercised, and the experience of others consulted. Good water is an essential blessing at sea; and it is only when we find it bad, that we are fully taught its value. The same may with equal propriety be said of every enjoyment in life; " for he who the storm has never defied, can scarce enjoy the calm." From a variety of fortuitous circumstances incidental to a long voyage, it is not only necessary to be sparing in the allowance, but that every abuse of it be prevented. The water we had was far from being agree-
                                                            able

able to the taste, and by no means improved by being long kept, which I am told is the case with Thames water. A great deal depends on the proper seasoning of the casks; —if new, the water is apt to retain a taste of the wood. The filtering stone, which most ships now provide themselves with, is peculiarly useful. The process of filtering takes away the rank fœtid smell which water long kept at sea generally has. With equal advantage we might adopt a method of purifying this element, as practised by the Chinese, on the authority of Sir George Staunton's late embassy to China.—" The Chinese put a small piece of alum in the hollow tube of a cane, which is perforated with small holes; with this instrument the muddy water is stirred a few minutes, and the earthy particles being speedily precipitated, leave the water above them pure and clear."

Nothing so forcibly struck me as the degree of neglect, and harsh treatment, which the Lascar sailors meet with on board. In cold climates they are quite inactive and inanimate; but, on entering a warm latitude, their

their motions become proportionably rapid, and their exertions more useful.

The slow pacing clouds have become more settled and fixed to the horizon; and from amidst their collected mass, we fondly expect the aspiring cliffs of Africa will speedily terminate our voyage, in which hope I shall for the present bid my friend adieu.

LETTER II.

Mountainous prospect on approaching the Cape---Sterility of Table Mountain---False Bay---A storm---The general joy on hearing " land in sight" proclaimed---Cast anchor in Simon's Bay---Village of Simon's Town---Curiosity of strangers in a foreign country---Description of the capital of the Cape---Its buildings---Inhabitants, their religion---Climate---Government ---A fashionable resort---Villas in the neighbourhood---Tremendous gales common in Table Bay---Dreadful effects of them.

AN assemblage of bleak and barren mountains form the outlines of the prospect on approaching the Cape. The celebrated Table Mountain exhibits an awful picture of bold projecting rocks, and parched sterility. No lively verdure catches the eager sight; in vain we look around for the flowery meads of this fertile colony.

It was on the evening of the 8th of June when we made the land; during the night

it

it was almost a calm; the unruffled face of
the ocean, that seemed for a while to forget
its tempestuous rage, and the glimmering of
the moon on its glossy surface, in conjunc-
tion with the gloomy pile of mountains towards which we gradually tended, formed a
sublime and impressive scene!   Early next
morning we found ourselves close in with
False Bay, and from the appearance on all
sides, a change in the weather was to be
dreaded. The surrounding mountains were
hid from our sight, and the lowering clouds
seemed to forebode a storm. Almost in the
very harbour, to be thus in danger of being
driven out to sea, and again made the sport
of winds and waves, struck a damp on our
spirits. Towards mid-day the storm increased; the rain poured upon us in torrents
without intermission for the greatest part of
the day, and the genius of the Table Mountain seemed as if resolved to prevent our
landing. In the evening the gale mode-
rated, and we again anticipated the pleasure
of getting rid of the cares and inconveniences
of ship-board. By him who has been for
months cooped up in a ship, and to whom
                                        day

View of Linon's Bay.

Engraved from Drawings made from Nature by the Author.

Pub. Nov. 1. 1816 by James Candin, Albion Press, London.

day after day the face of nature has been continually the same, by him alone can the gaiety and happy expressions of the countenances of all on board be conceived, when the mariner from the mast-head proclaims aloud the joyful cry of *land in sight*. We hailed it as an old friend with whom we have enjoyed the happiest moments of our lives; and in our first transports of congratulation, the barren rocks possess charms equally attractive with the most highly cultivated fields. On the morning of the 9th we anchored in Simon's Bay, which was crowded with ships from all quarters of the globe. The winter season having set in, it was no longer safe for ships to remain in Table Bay. The village of Simon's Town, running along the beach, almost at the foot of the overhanging mountains, presented a gay and picturesque appearance, rendered still more striking when contrasted with the dreary prospect of the surrounding country.

When a new page in the volume of nature is, as it were, laid open before us, impelled by a spirit of novelty, we are hurried from the contemplation of one object to that of another,

another, with hardly a moment left for reflection; prompted by a laudable curiosity, we wander over the diversified scene with emotions of pleasure, at one time pleasingly employed in observing the different appearances in the newly discovered land, and at another time the customs, habits, and manners of those among whom we are going to reside.

To attempt, after the numerous descriptions with which the world has been amused, to lay before you my poor picture of Southern Africa, may be deemed somewhat presumptuous; it is, indeed, pursuing a hackneyed path; still, though the harvest has been already gathered in, the *industrious gleaner* may have it in his power to collect some *neglected ears* that lie scattered around. With this humble hope I shall cheerfully engage in the delightful task of wandering from field to field, and from flower to flower. After the labors of the day, permit me to present my *collected sheaves* at the shrine of friendship, and may the unvitiated palate of my friend be inclined to partake of my sober meal.

The

The capital of the Cape is a neat, regular, well built town, and occupies a greater extent of ground than is generally imagined; —it contains some handsome buildings, but, from the prevalence of violent winds, they are generally built low. They make use of clay as mortar, and give a coating of plaister to the outside when finished;—this is decorated according to the taste and fancy of the builder; the doors and windows generally painted green, a favorite color with the Dutch.

A stone terrace, extending the whole length of the house, and elevated a few feet above the level of the street, is the grand promenade of the family; this is called the *Stoop;* and towards evening it is commonly thronged with visitors. Mynheer seats himself at one end of it, enjoying the luxury of his tobacco, and with apparent unconcern eyes the passing throng.

There are two churches within the town, and the religion of the inhabitants is that of the reformed church, the calvinists being the most numerous. In the external duties of religion they are sufficiently zealous, and regular

regular attendants of church on Sundays; but in the after part of the day, when the exercises of devotion are finished, it is no unusual thing among the young ladies to form parties of pleasure, and spend the evening in the ball-room.

Though now the middle of winter, or, as it may be termed with greater propriety, the wet season, yet, when the sky is clear, the influence of the meridian sun is still powerful; but suddenly it becomes remarkably cold, and a person is at a loss how to clothe himself, for the transitions from heat to cold, and from cold to heat, can hardly be equalled in any other climate. Sore-throats, and similar complaints, are the natural consequences of these sudden changes.

The Government Garden situated at the higher part of the valley, which forms an amphitheatre, is a fashionable resort in the cool of the evening; and when the scorching rays of a summer's sun render every other place about town unpleasant and oppressive, here one may enjoy a delightful coolness under the shade of the spreading oaks. It is about a quarter of an hour's walk

walk from the top to the bottom. It has been lately inclosed with a brick wall. In the immediate neighbourhood there are some charming villas, although, from the aridity of the soil, and the consequent want of water, these cultivated spots do not extend to any considerable distance from the town.

At this season we naturally look for those tremendous gales from the north-west, which render Table Bay the terror of seamen from the month of May to September: indeed, from a recent mournful event, we are apt to believe, that no season is secure from those storms which blow from the Western Ocean, and that roll into this ill-fated bay those destructive billows, which carry along with them ruin and dismay.

The last melancholy spectacle of the kind which the inhabitants had an opportunity of witnessing, was on the 5th of November, 1799. Nature at times delights in departing from that systematic order, by which mankind presume to fetter her operations. When least expected, she breaks from her trammels,

trammels, and shews that the boasted wisdom of man is nought but vanity.

His Majesty's ship Sceptre was unfortunately one of the sufferers on the occasion. Soon after the salute in commemoration of the King's birth-day, the canon's roar spoke a different language than that of rejoicing; it conveyed to the soul the deep hollow groans of distress; the storm increased apace as the evening approached; a dark night succeeded, to add, if it were possible, to the horrors of the scene; and the shrieks of the dying were borne on the wings of the roaring winds, until the awful catastrophe was at length completed. The following morning presented a distressing sight, the miserable remains of the vessel, and the mangled bodies of the dead half-buried in the sand! Here let me pause. May the arrogant be taught humility, and the compassionate bosom sympathize with suffering humanity.— Leaving my friend to the enjoyment of those feelings which the tragical recital is calculated to excite, I remain, &c.

Engraved from Drawings made from Nature by the Author.

A Bullock-waggon of Hottentot Holland, crossing a Mountain.

LETTER III.

Superiority of the waggon-drivers---Oxen commonly employed
---The horses chiefly of Spanish breed---Their peculiar pace
---Races established by the garrison---Dutch ladies ride in
covered waggons---Cruelty of the English in lopping off the
tails of their horses---Characteristics of the Dutch---English
manners adopted, particularly by the ladies---Their levity and
familiarity accounted for.

THE dexterity which the waggon-drivers
at the Cape display in the management of
their horses, cannot fail to be remarked by
the European on his arrival. Seated in the
front of his waggon, he can with astonishing
precision strike with his long whip any part of
the animal that he pleases. Eight in hand, he
can direct, seemingly with as much ease, as
if there were only two in the yoke, let the
road be steep or rugged, or the turnings
ever so sudden, yet in all the intricacies of
driving,

driving, and the nice management of the whip, his superiority to the European is universally acknowledged. Such as are destined for this employment are early instructed in the rudiments of the art, and from the time that the young colonist can make use of his hands, his favorite amusement is to handle the whip, and to charm his ears with its music. From its length it requires both hands to guide it; and its cracking is heard at a considerable distance. In their heavy draught waggons they employ oxen, which convey from the distant parts of the interior the produce of the land to the Cape market. The team commonly consists of twelve or sixteen. The two leading oxen are always the best, and most tractable. A Hottentot boy runs at their head, to guide them in the road, and to assist the driver. The oxen that perform these long journeys are well looking cattle, with large, branching horns. While they travel in the dry season, it may naturally be supposed that from fatigue, want of care, and the parched tracts of country they must necessarily pass through, they cannot be

in

in good condition on their arrival at the Cape.

The horses of the colony are not remarkable for strength or shape; they are mostly of the Spanish kind, imported from the opposite continent, by no means deficient in spirit, and well calculated for undergoing fatigue. They have a peculiar pace, which is called *the bungher*, but when once they come under the hands of an English jockey, they soon get rid of it. Since the possession of the Cape by the English, the breed of horses has been now attended to, and materially improved. The races, which have been established by the garrison, have contributed greatly to this end;—they are regularly held twice a-year, and continue a week at each time. The prizes are made up by subscription, and excellent sport is frequently to be met with. The Dutch ladies ride in covered waggons, and animate the scene by an assemblage of beauty and fashion.

A Dutchman cannot easily reconcile himself to lopping off the tail of his *paard*. On passing from a Dutch to an English master, the

the poor animal immediately finds himself robbed of his long tail, which, in the eyes of his former master, appeared not less ornamental than useful. Attached to the customs of our country, we are but too apt to overlook, in an implicit compliance with them, the comfort of an animal that so essentially contributes to our profit and pleasure. Vast number of flies, during the hot season, incessantly teaze, and torment the horses of this country; it is, therefore, a barbarous practice to deprive them (especially here) of an appendage which bountiful nature has furnished them with as the best means in repelling the attacks of those troublesome visitors. When annoyed by swarms of flies, I have frequently seen them writhing and distorting the part of the tail left them, as if to reproach the cruelty of their new masters!

The Cape is no longer that cheap country as it has been formerly represented; and I may even venture to assert, that the ideas which are generally entertained of this part of the world, are far from being correct. The gay illusion passes from hand to hand, and

and the southern part of Africa is painted as a paradise.

Industry has been always held up to us as a prominent feature in the character of a Dutchman; but I am afraid this characteristic of the mother-country is not so well supported in Africa.

At a general survey, you would be inclined to pronounce the inhabitants indolent and inactive; or, at least, where exertions are discovered, they are comparatively trifling, and confined to narrow bounds. I shall not, however, be too forward in exhibiting a picture, which requires more leisure, a longer residence in the country, and better opportunities, than I yet can boast of. I shall cheerfully, with a strict and inviolable regard to truth, endeavour to amuse my friend from time to time with my Gleanings in the physical, moral, or intellectual world, and in the prosecution of this,

——" Nothing extenuate,
Nor aught set down in malice.

English manners begin more and more to prevail;

prevail; but it seems the peculiar province of the fair sex to copy after the fashions of our country. The Cape ladies possess an elegance in their manners, and a degree of symmetry in their persons, conjoined to an agreeable expression of countenance, which cannot fail to attract our regard. No doubt that portion of levity and familiarity which has been ascribed to them, in a great measure arises from their intercourse with strangers, for, to the same intercourse, from the first establishment of the colony to the present time, their manners have assumed that mixed character which holds a kind of equipoise between Dutch composure, and French frivolity.

The plant that quickly arrives at maturity, is found in the same proportion to hasten to decay; this reasoning is found applicable to the Cape ladies. That beauty which only blows and blossoms, early dies and fades away. When this climacteric period approaches, they begin to assume that roundness of figure which evinces their original stamp. At some future period I shall
probably

probably extend this part of my picture:—
here I have given you only the outlines:
—the varied colors, and requisite shades,
shall in good time be furnished by

Yours, &c.

LETTER IV.

Cabos del Tormentos---Beautiful heaths between Table and False Bay---A diversity of charming flowers---Their vegetation quick---The flowers succeeded every month by different ones---Neat villas and rich plantations---A kind of sameness in the laying out of their pleasure-grounds---The cultivation of the vine chiefly attended to in the neighbourhood of the town---The sale of firewood another source of advantage---The slaves employed in conveying it to town---The silver-tree ---The Scotch fir---The price of board and lodging, &c. increased since the establishment of the English---Butchers' meat cheap---Fish plenty---Table Bay frequented by whales in winter---The whale-fishery.

THE Portuguese were not far wrong in naming this promontory of Africa *Cabos del Tormentos,* (Cape of Plagues,) from the storms and tempests frequently encountered by their early navigators. I should be inclined to allot this part of the world as a proper residence for Eolus in the early ages of of heathen mythology; but when it opened a passage to the treasures of the east, these avaricious adventurers, in honor to the discovery, gave it the name it now bears.

In my walks I am delighted with the variety of beautiful heaths, that almost cover the extensive tract of flat country between Table and False Bay. The geranium is seen to grow almost from the sand, besides a diversity of the most charming flowers, ' *that waste their sweetness in the desert air.*' I must confess myself ignorant of botany; and though, in my early days, I ventured to pursue its flowery path, yet, never did I experience till now the poignancy of regret, in having neglected so pleasing a study. The exhaustless stores of nature lie open before me, and I can only admire the beauteous collection, without being able to ascertain their several charms. But may we not enjoy pleasures of a superior kind, though ignorant of the minutiæ of a science to which they may belong? It does not require a knowledge of anatomy to discover the fine proportions of a well-formed body; nor is it, in my opinion, absolutely essential to understand

stand botany, to derive pleasure from a well cultivated garden. June, July, and August, are the months at the Cape best suited to the excursions of the botanist, this being the rainy season. A succession of beautiful and charming flowers may be said to follow every shower; their vegetation is quick, and they in a manner start into existence. Every flower has its own particular season. When those of one month wither and disappear, the succeeding month produces others, differing in form, and variety of colors, from those that just preceded them; and this, perhaps, happens in almost the same spot. —This agreeable phenomenon I have more than once had occasion to observe.

When I cast my eyes around, I fancy myself in the depth of winter. The bleak and dreary appearance of the surrounding country, the naked oak, now shivering with every blast, form a kind of an unnatural group amidst the beauties I have been attempting to describe.

On the east side of the Table Mountain, and stretching along the bottom of it, a landscape of neat villas and rich plantations

is

is exhibited to the view. Myrtle and oak
hedges inclose their vineyards. In the vicinity of their houses, a few large, full grown
oaks are to be seen; but at this season they
are stripped of their foliage, and while the
naked trees proclaim the reign of winter,
you have only to cast your eyes to the flowers
on every side; and you will discover evident
marks of a forward spring. Thus, my friend,
spring and winter join hands, and become
united. In the laying out of their pleasure-
grounds, a kind of sameness prevails throughout, and the national character stands prominent,—every tree and shrub is so disposed
as to form *a straight line,* from which the
African Dutchman never deviates. In the
immediate neighbourhood of the town, the
cultivation of the vine, and the improvement
of their gardens, from which they derive
very considerable profits, occupy their chief
attention.—Another source of advantage is
in the sale of fire-wood. What the colonists
call the Kreupel Boom, and seemingly
adapted for no other use, is what they mostly
cut down for this purpose. They employ
their slaves in carrying it to town across
their

their shoulders;—probably, when I find a leisure moment, I shall call your attention to this unfortunate class of our fellow-creatures at the Cape.

The silver-tree, which, I believe, is peculiar to the Cape, is so named from its beautiful white foliage; it is generally known by the name of the *Wittle Boom.* The finest plantations of these are to be seen in the vicinity of Constantia. I have remarked that the Scotch fir is here vigorous and healthy; and should the Larix be introduced, I make no doubt of its thriving equally as well. It may probably, at some future period, be thought not unworthy the consideration of government, (as a matter of colonial importance,) to bestow some attention to the plantation of trees here; to be guided in their operations by a proper encouragement to the planting of such only as are best suited to the soil and climate, and to pitch upon situations least exposed to those violent winds that prevail throughout the year. At present, great quantities of wood are conveyed in small coasting vessels from Mossil Bay to Cape town. An increasing

creasing population will occasion an increased consumption of so essential an article; and only by the adoption of timely measures, can every apprehension of future society be entirely removed.

It seems to be a natural consequence attending the settlement of the English in any part of the world, to advance materially the price of the produce of whatever country they reside in. At the Cape it has been peculiarly the case, and the Dutch settlers are ever ready to acknowledge it. Every article of living may be said to be tripled since their arrival. Board and lodging, which, while under the Dutch government, could be had for about a rix-dollar a day, can now hardly be procured for two;—every thing has suffered a proportional increase. The single article of butcher's meat is, indeed, cheap. Nature has also acted her part, by storing the surrounding bays with variety of excellent fish, such as the steen brash, Hottentot, and Roman fish; the latter, esteemed the most delicate of all, is caught only in False Bay.

In

In the winter months Table Bay is frequented by whales, and they sometimes approach very near to the shore. The fishery is rather on the decline; but is still carried on with considerable success. The average fishing of a season is about sixteen whales, and a few of them measure seventy feet in length. There is a house erected near the shore for cutting up and manufacturing the blubber. Eighteen leagers of oil, of about one hundred and fifty-four gallons each, is what is commonly produced from a good whale. A leager of oil generally fetches eighty rix-dollars.

I shall not apologize for the brevity of this letter, as my communications shall always be constant: the task of gleaning for a friend is particularly delightful; and as I mean soon to resume it, for the present I must bid adieu.

Engraved from Drawings made from Nature by the Author.

Whale Fishing near the Cape.

Pub. Sec. 1809. by Vernor Hood & Sharpe, London.

LETTER V.

Visits from the hyena at night---Terror of the dogs at his ap-
proach---The farmer's snare for taking them alive---The uncommon strength, and chief residence of these animals---
Reasons for expecting their total extirpation---The country
favorable for sportsmen---The manner a colonist travels when
on a shooting party---A farmer prefers oxen to horses---Re-
markable birds---A society instituted for the encouragement
of agriculture---A scarcity of corn---Remarks thereon.

IT is from the east side of the Table
Mountain that I again address my friend.
Here we enjoy the cool, refreshing breeze
wafted from the southern ocean. At night
the hyena pays us a visit, and prowls around
our camp. He gives notice of his approach
by his hoarse and plaintive howlings. When
the dogs find their enemy is at hand, they
set up an hideous howling, expressive of
their terror, and this mingled concert of discordant

cordant sounds banishes all sleep from the
eye-lids. When the hyena boldly advances,
the barking of the dogs suddenly ceases, and
they remain in silent terror at his approach.
The farmers in our neighbourhood lay a
snare for taking them alive, which is a simple contrivance. A building of about six
feet square, and as many feet in height,
open at top, with a sliding door, is all that
seems necessary for the purpose. The bait
that attracts them is placed within, and fixed
in such a manner, that on their attempting
to devour it, the door falls down instanta-
neously, and thus they become prisoners.
I have seen one caught in this manner;
—it was the spotted wolf, which I believe
to be the common hyena of the Cape. Our
farmer called it the *Cape Bear;* indeed, the
name seems sufficiently appropriate, for they
bear no small resemblance to that animal in
their form.

He mentioned at the same time, that the
hyena possesses uncommon strength in its
head, and that the most violent and repeated
blows on that part could hardly deprive it of
life. I have seen it attacked by an English
bull-

Manner of Catching the Hyena.

Engraved from Drawings made from Nature by the Author.

bull-dog with the most savage ferocity, but its hard, tough skin was impenetrable to the teeth of his opponent. The hyenas take up their abode amidst the rugged cliffs of the Table Mountain, and along that chain of mountains running in a southerly direction, till they terminate in what we may with propriety call Cape Point. At times they are met with by the traveller at night, on the road leading from *Wynberg* to Cape Town, but are never sufficiently daring to venture an attack. It is no uncommon thing to hear of their falling upon strayed oxen and horses, and when left alone in any sequestered spot, there remains little chance of their escaping.

These ravenous animals in the neighbourhood of the Cape, will, perhaps, at no very distant period, be totally extirpated, and only be met with in the more solitary regions of the interior. The tract of country they are now in, was doubtless at some former period frequented by the lion, tiger, and hippopotamus, and the rest of these savage quadrupeds that have receded from the approach of man. It is, perhaps, not altogether

altogether fanciful to suppose, that traces
may be discovered of their once inhabiting
the country around us. At no great distance
there is a district called Tigerberg, where,
at present, the appearance of a tiger is somewhat rare; also, about eight miles hence,
there is a lake that still retains the name of
the *Sea-cow Lake*, though these huge mon-
sters no longer disturb its repose.—The encroachments of man cause the savage tribe
to recede.

The *Steen-bok* and *Grys-bok* spring from
the thickets on every side. Jackalls and
hares are also numerous, and this country is
peculiarly favorable to the pursuits of the
sportsman. When a colonist goes on a
shooting party, he travels in a light cart
made for the purpose, and he can thus carry
along with him every conveniency suited to
the journey. Seated in his waggon, with
his gun by his side, he is driven along with
rapidity. When the game is started, he
stops his vehicle, and can then with coolness take his aim. Many of the farmers,
when they have a mind to partake of this
amusement, prefer oxen to horses, as the
slow,

Engraved from Drawing made from Nature by the Author.

Shooting the Steen Bok, in the Neighbourhood of the Cape.

Pub. Nov. 1806. by James Candee, Ivy Lane Pater. Noster Row, London.

slow, deliberate pace of the former is, in their opinion, better calculated for ensuring sport, than the quick ambling step of the latter.

We have already been furnished with an accurate account of the ornithology of this part of Africa from the labours and researches of *Vaillant.* The feathered tribe here are more noted for variety and beauty of plumage, than for sweetness in their notes. The golden snipe of the Cape is a beautiful bird; it differs in nothing material from the common snipe, except in the spotted brightness of its wings. The paradise swallow has received a tint of colouring from the hand of nature, which the most exquisite pencil could hardly pourtray. It is a bird of passage, and commonly makes its appearance on the approach of the warm season. It seems fond of trees, and towards evening retires among the branches to repose during the night.

A society has lately been instituted in the colony for the encouragement of agriculture, and the arts and sciences; premiums have been offered for the amelioration of their wines,

wines, and a more approved mode recom-
mended. The grapes of the Cape are allowed to be equal to those of the southern
countries of Europe, but in the happy art of
making a proper use of this rich gift of
nature, they are, indeed, miserably inferior
to them.

The scarcity of corn which England has
of late so severely felt, has with rapid strides
visited us in Africa. What! methinks I
hear my friend exclaim,—the Cape threatened with famine,—that magazine of plenty,
the garden of the world! This is in fact
the case, and sickly want begins to stare us
in the face. We are already restricted to a
ration of half a pound of bread per day, as
if the whole colony had been ordered on a
voyage of discovery to the south pole. During the time of the Dutch government, a
failure in the crops was provided against, by
storing up the superabundance of plentiful
years. This wise policy has hitherto been
neglected by the English, and the present
scarcity speaks loudly in its favor. There is
frequently a species of false alarm, so closely
connected with a scarcity of corn in all countries,

tries, that we find it difficult to ascertain the fact, or the genuine grounds for erecting it, but once excited, it spreads like wildfire, and the whole herd of forestallers profit by the the alarm. If, however, this necessary article cannot be procured, as usual, at a reasonable price, we may pronounce it *scarce;* but it should certainly be inquired into, whether providence has ordained such scarcity for the correction of national prodigality, or whether it proceeds from illegal monopoly; and if it can be discovered, (as I believe it was the case in England,) that heaven was bountiful, but man was avaricious, no punishment can be too great for those base wretches on earth who dare to withhold the blessings from above, and attribute to providence the distress which they themselves occasion!

My gleanings increase apace;—if they chance in the least to contribute to your amusement, or to pass agreeably away some of those tedious hours which few of us are without, then, indeed, I shall have attained my end. Methinks I hear the whispering voice of friendship bid me go on.—Yes,
amidst

amidst the noon-tide heat and evening shade, I shall cheerfully glean my way. May the winds prove propitious, and waft them safely to you. In the mean time,

Adieu.

LETTER VI.

Table Bay not a safe harbour---A curious phenomenon respecting it in some degree accounted for---The sublimity of an approaching south-east wind---Seldom or ever accompanied with rain---The weather succeeding it generally hot---Salubrity of the winds during summer---This season always in extremes---The evenings generally cool---The manner in which the Dutch exclude the heat from their rooms---Their buildings excel in decorations, and their towns in cleanliness---Stoves used in winter---Their propensity to parade.

THE south-east winds have set in, and Table Bay is again the rendezvous of the shipping; perhaps, at no season, can it strictly be said to be a secure and safe harbour. A violent south-east wind may at times endanger the shipping, by causing them to run foul of each other, or part from their moorings, and may drive them out to sea. At times you may perceive the north side of
this

this bay agitated with a strong south-east
wind; while the south side, or that next the
town, seems hardly to feel its impression;—
at the same moment a ship is seen going out
with a fair wind on the north side, when, on
the south side, another may be seen coming
in enjoying a like advantage. This curious
phenomenon may, in some degree, be accounted for. From the lower part of the
Table Mountain, which terminates to the
north-east in what is generally known by
the name of *The Devil's Hill*, the south-east
wind is first felt, and its approach announced
by the curl upon the water in that part of
the bay that is immediately opposite. This
same wind, in its direction from the Indian
ocean, is opposed by the promontory of the
Cape, where, meeting with opposition, it
directs its course along the intermediate bays
on the west side, till it reaches Table Bay,
where, acting thus partially, the wind seems
to blow from the westward. It is only on
the commencement of a south-east wind that
this is to be observed, as the increasing violence of the wind soon overpowers the partial breeze from the westward.

I have

I have frequently with no small degree of pleasure contemplated the sublime picture of an approaching south-east wind,—marked its commencement and progress, and felt all the littleness of man in the grandeur of the scene! A thin, white vapour, seems at first to attach itself to the highest part of the mountain; it gradually becomes larger, and as it increases in size, the wind is proportionally violent. This congregated mass of vapour in a little time covers the summit of the mountain, and is big with the impending storm. No clouds obscure the sky, and the sun remains as bright as on the clearest day. This artillery of the mountain is quickly set in motion; the white fleecy clouds roll majestically along, and cling to the rugged cliffs. By degrees they acquire accumulated force, and are driven with impetuosity along the valley below. Columns of dust are whirled in the air, and the ships at anchor in the bay boldly bid defiance to the storm.

The south-east winds are seldom or never accompanied with rain; a drizzling, damp vapour is sometimes felt in the immediate neighbourhood

neighbourhood of the mountain. When this wind blows hot, it is extremely disagreeable, and apt to occasion languor, and depression of the animal spirits. At the season when they are most prevalent and violent, (that is from November to the month of February,) they continue to blow for three or four days without any intermission. They slacken about mid-day, but, towards evening, recommence with redoubled fury. The weather that succeeds the south-east wind is generally hot in the extreme.

Those winds that invariably blow during the summer season from the south-east, must essentially contribute to the salubrity of the climate, and are a powerful preservation of health. Nothing can withstand their violence, and all the noxious effluvia arising from the butchers' shops, and those pools which lie close to the doors of the inhabitants, are thereby happily dissipated.

The summer weather of the Cape is always in extremes, either with violent winds, or scorching heat; but the evenings are generally cool, and delightfully serene. The rays of an ever bright sun, reflected from the

the craggy side of the Table Mountain, are here concentrated, and, together with the glare from the white houses, add greatly to the heat experienced in Cape Town. The Dutch exclude the external heat by darkening their rooms, and you always feel a refreshing coolness on entering them.

In external appearance, and fanciful decoration in their buildings, these people indeed excel; and few towns can boast of superior neatness and cleanliness. In winter they make use of stoves; not many, however, can boast of the comforts of a snug fire-side. In the arrangement of their furniture, perhaps, we may discover a propensity to parade and shew. Here I cannot help remarking, that when an Englishman travels, the strong prejudices of his country ever attend him; and, when in the course of his researches, any marked difference from the customs and manners of his country is perceived, he is but too apt to stigmatize it with the name of error, and consider it as an aberration from propriety.

To

To follow up my plan with assiduity and perseverance, so becoming the character I have assumed, shall be my utmost endeavour; while, with every sentiment of respect,

I am, &c.

LETTER VII.

Introduction to a Caffre chief---His hospitable reception---Description of his dress---The apparent gratitude and pleasure of his interpreter on recognizing a British officer, whose prisoner he had been---The peculiar shrill whistle of the Caffres ---The chief's stature, features, &c.---Their present king--- Necessity of establishing a friendly intercourse with them--- Enmity of the Boors of the more distant parts of the colony--- The Caffres made their dupes---Tranquillity restored by the vigorous measures of government---The most rebellious Boors imprisoned.

I HAVE been highly gratified by having been introduced to the presence of a Caffre chief, who had accompanied a Dutch gentleman from Caffraria, in order to pay his respects to His Excellency the Governor of the Cape. He entered the room with a dignified step, and seemed neither startled nor abashed on being brought before a crowded

crowded company. Wine and fruit were presented him, which he accepted with apparent satisfaction; his eyes glistened with delight on viewing the table and the guests. All evinced a pleasing emulation in paying court to this swarthy son of Africa, by every mark of attention which might convey favorable impressions of the British character. On returning to his country and government, he could not fail to make known the hospitable reception, and kind treatment which he met with at the Cape.

It was no bad policy for the government to make friends of such a brave and enterprising race of men, and may eventually be attended with the happiest consequences.

The dress of our chief was of that kind, that seemed ill-calculated for the parade of the drawing-room. It brought to recollection the primeval state of man, when his wants were few, and easily satisfied. His head-dress consisted of a plume of ostrich feathers, fastened by a brass fillet; his body wrapped round with the skin of a tiger, with the rough side turned inwards. A brass girdle encircled the lower part of it. He wore

Engraved from Drawings made from Nature by the Author.

A Caffre Chief attacking a Lion.

Pub. Nov. 1. 1805, by James Cundee, Albion Press, London.

wore three large ivory bracelets on his left
arm, which latter is, among the Caffres, an
honorable mark of distinction, being the
badge of merit, or reward of prowess. The
killing of a lion, or an elephant, is sometimes
honored with an additional ring of ivory.
It fits closely to the arm, and has received
a very neat polish from their hands.

It was rumoured at the Cape that he was
Angola, a brave and enterprising chief, who
had distinguished himself in the late Caffre
war. He was attended by an interpreter,
who, being formerly in the service of a
Dutch Boor, had acquired their language.
This attendant recognised an officer present,
whom he had seen on duty in the wilds of
Africa; he had been taken prisoner by the
British troops, and mildly dealt with;—even
at this distance of time, his countenance
seemed expressive of mingled gratitude and
pleasure in beholding a face that seemed
familiar to him. I could fancy him busily
employed in giving an account of his capture to his chief, by his pointing with his
finger to the officer as he spoke. The Caffres
whistle in a peculiar shrill manner, and are
                                        heard

heard at a considerable distance. As to
these little traits of character in an almost
unknown race of men, you will readily pardon my giving them to you as they presented
themselves in this interesting moment.

The Caffres are in general tall, muscular,
and athletic; the present subject of my
gleanings was not much above the middle
size of Europeans. A conscious air of freedom that marked his different movements,
an animated countenance that indicated penetration and discernment, added to a certain dignity of manner, composed a *tout
ensemble* peculiarly suited to the character
of a free nation. They had not the narrow
visage, nor prominent cheek-bones of the
Hottentot, but, upon the whole, bore a
nearer resemblance to an European countenance. The present king of the Caffres is
Gaica; he has under him a number of inferior chiefs, who acknowledge his authority, and who are ever ready to obey his
commands.—The establishing of a friendly
intercourse between those respective independent chiefs, and the government at the
Cape, ought surely not to be neglected. To
                                        prevent

prevent the encroachments of the Boors on the frontiers of the colony, and to check those multiplied violations of their natural rights, which by the Dutch colonist have been but too often practised with impunity, are measures of sound policy.

The late disturbances that took place in the Cape country, which required the interposition of the strong arm of government to suppress, is well known to have been fomented and encouraged by the Boors of the more distant parts of the colony, aided and abetted by the insidious machinations of a few residents at the Cape. The Caffres were made the dupes of their mingled cunning and treachery, and brought forward to sustain the brunt of the war. Far removed from the seat of government, those incendiaries flattered themselves that they were beyond the reach of punishment, and that they might with perfect security, amid the wilds of Africa, bid defiance to colonial laws and regulations, and sound the trumpet of rebellion. Many of those demi-savages of Africa deserted their families and houses on the approach of the British troops, fearing

ing the punishment due to their crimes, and being excellent marksmen, who could easily annoy the march of regular troops, they carried on an irregular kind of warfare.

In the same manner, we may easily conceive, did the Caffres carry on their operations;—they sometimes made their appearance in numerous bodies, advancing slowly in the form of a wedge. Concealed in their woods and fastnesses, they acted with more effect; and from their superior knowledge of the country, were at times successful against a few straggling parties of British troops. These transactions are so involved in uncertainty and obscurity, that we cannot pretend to remove the veil. Notwithstanding the fatiguing marches, in pursuing the steps of an ever active enemy, ready to take advantage of their followers, and letting no occasion slip when they might dart their assigays with effect, the vigorous and decisive measures of government, in a short time restored the tranquillity of the country. The possessions of the Caffres were acknowledged and secured to them. Such of those infatuated Boors who were most forward in fomenting discontent,

discontent, and in exciting opposition, were made prisoners, and marched to the Cape, where they still remain in confinement. They must sensibly feel this sudden reverse of fortune, entailed upon themselves by their treacherous conduct to a brave race of men, as well as by an unnatural rebellion against a mild government. We here see, my friend, that the sequestered regions of Africa have not been exempt from the scourge of revolutionary principles, and the factious spirit of modern Europe.

I remain, &c.

LETTER VIII.

The condition of slavery considered---The Malay and Mosambique slaves---Their daily employment---Meagre fare---Slaves
often sold by auction---The colonists, particularly the ladies,
fond of frequenting those sales-- Consequent remarks.

IN a former letter I hinted my intention
of laying before you some particulars relative to the slaves of this colony, Unhappy
race! how often have you tottered under
the heavy burden imposed by your unfeeling masters! In contemplating your hard
lot among mankind, the generous bosom
will certainly experience those finer feelings
of our nature which ever accompany the
ardent wishes of thousands for your emancipation. Is complexion alone the grand characteristic of slavery? Since your swarthy
coloring

coloring was given you by our common parent, is it for this that you are doomed to be
hunted down in your calm retreats, torn
from your families and homes, and carried
by the trafficker in human flesh to the mart
of avarice? Though, for a while, the united
efforts of many celebrated characters have
proved fruitless in the abolition of this trade,
yet, still a gleam of hope pervades the philanthropic mind, that ere long the legislature
of a free and enlightened country will inter-
fere with redoubled energy in behalf of the
violated rights of humanity, and remove the
foul stain that blots the European character.
We ought ever to keep in mind, that what
is morally wrong, can never be politically
right. It has been asserted by many, that
the condition, and manner of treatment of
the slaves at the Cape, is better and preferable to that which they experience in other
European settlements. Are the Dutch settlers at the Cape more alive to the feelings
of humanity than those of other countries?
Are they more attentive to the little wants
of their slaves, or does a greater degree of
confidence subsist between both parties, than
is

is to be found elsewhere? Are their labors less severe, or less scrupulously exacted? While the characters of men are so various and diversified, those under their immediate control must experience, more or less, bad treatment, according to the different humors and tempers of their masters. The African planters are not, indeed, over burdened with these finer sensibilities of our nature, which at times occasion a few alterations from rectitude, yet often prove an exhaustless source of delight.

The Malay and Mosambique slaves principally compose those of the Cape. The former are distinguished by their copper color; and the latter by a jet black, and thick lips. The Malay, cruel and revengeful in his disposition, is allowed to possess a better capacity for instruction, and when taught a trade, becomes a source of profit to his master.—The Mosambique slave has a dull, inanimated appearance strongly stamped upon him, indicating, as it were, an inferiority of intellect. As these are less dangerous from the tameness of their nature, and more apt to become attached to their masters,

masters, they form a very numerous class of the Cape slaves.

A number of these poor wretches are daily employed in carrying burdens of firewood to town, borne across their shoulders. Towards evening the great road leading into town is crowded with returning slaves, almost exhausted under their loads. For this they travel about ten or twelve miles. It is astonishing with what ease they move under their burdens, and it is no unusual thing for them, to trundle them along the greatest part of the way. When they leave their master's house in the morning, they are provided with some bread, and *sheep's-tail* to supply the place of butter. A portion of dried fish is sometimes added, to enrich their repast. The wood that is thus conveyed to town, is either consumed in their master's family, or disposed of to his advantage. The harassed negro has probably next morning, at daybreak, the same journey to re-commence, furnished with the same meagre fare, and the same heavy burden to totter under. Such runaway slaves, as have taken refuge amidst the rugged caverns of the neighbouring

ing mountains, are fed by their companions
from town, who willingly share with them
their scanty meal.

Among the ills incidental to a state of
slavery, we may take into the account, that
of passing from one master to another. Here
there is an ever-shifting scene of all kinds
of property, and the poor slave is destined to
experience a similar transfer. On the em-
barrassment, or death of his master, it may
indeed sometimes happen, that the slave
profits by the change, but this is regulated
by the chapter of accidents. Numbered
among the live-stock of the family, upon
the death of their masters, they are immediately handed about in the bill of sale, and
when sold, the profits are as quickly laid
hold of by the remaining branches of the
family, in their eagerness to share the property left them. Age and length of service,
domestic attachments, or any other binding
ties, are but too often totally disregarded.
No considerations of this kind can secure
them from coming to the hammer. It is
common to behold aged parents, with their
families around them, exposed to public ven-
dition.

dition. The colonists at the Cape seem
remarkably fond of frequenting those sales
which constitute, in the opinion of many,
one of their chief amusements. The ladies
possess an equal desire of resorting to them,
and are not scrupulously delicate in observing those pitiable objects in a state of
nudity. Would the ladies of our country
acquire any degree of enjoyment in witnessing scenes of this kind? I flatter myself not.
However willing to allow the Cape ladies
credit for every personal charm, yet I cannot avoid remarking, that (in my humble
apprehension) the accustoming themselves
to such barbarous spectacles, must in some
manner tend to eradicate those finer feelings
of our nature so peculiarly apposite and becoming the female character. The glistening
eye of sensibility, that gives its willing tribute to the scene of sorrow, or to the tale of
woe, possesses in itself something of a charm
far more attractive than the happiest assemblage of external beauties accompanying a
callous or unfeeling heart.

Adieu.

LETTER IX.

The subject continued---Beauty of the female slaves---Their love
of dress, &c.---An intercourse between them and their masters
rendered the source of profit---Daughters of families exposed
to danger by these attendants---Severity of the Dutch masters
---Riches can palliate the most heinous crimes---Slaves consti‑
tute the entire support of the families to which they belong---
Anecdote of a planter and a slave boy.

I RESUME the subject of my last letter,
for I remember well, when about to leave
the happy shores of Britain, where freedom
reigns, and to depart for the southern extremity of Africa, the benevolence of your
mind prompted you to request that I would
make such observations on the state of the
slaves in this colony as my situation might
enable me.   From the influence of early
prejudices, together with the ideas of our
riper

riper years, we are less apt to consider it as a crime, that a class of men, differing in complexion from ourselves, should for a series of ages have been condemned to slavery. When, in our intercourse with the world, we observe their sufferings, and the burdens imposed upon them, we easily persuade ourselves, that their inferiority in the scale of beings, justifies the exercise of severity towards them, and sanctions the traffic in human flesh; but when we see condemned to a state of slavery such as approximate the color of Europeans, we naturally become alarmed, and feel it as an insult offered to our species. What has led me into these reflections, is the number of the latter description to be met with at the Cape. From the fair European to the black Mosambique, you will perceive every intermediate gradation of color;—to this we may add a variety of features blended together, partaking, in some degree, the characteristic traits of the vast assemblage of different tribes and nations to be met with at the Cape.

The

The female slaves are particularly fair in their complexions, and are not destitute of charms to the sensual eye. Fond of dress, and equally ambitious to attract attention, they are seen on a Sunday parading the streets in all the tawdry finery of a modern courtezan. From their connection with Europeans, which is connived at by their masters, we need no longer be surprized at the fairness of their complexions. An intercourse of this kind becomes a profitable concern to the master of the family, by an addition (if we may be allowed the expression) to his live-stock. Amidst this field of libertinism, it frequently happens that the daughters of the family are not entirely exempt from danger. Being constantly attended by these female slaves, who enjoy their confidence, and enter into habits of familiarity with them, they unavoidably become a dangerous snare to entrap the young mind;—thus the bias they receive in their youth, progressively expands into those little indelicacies of sentiment and manners, that by them open to misconstruction, and the censure of the world.

The

The Dutch have been rarely behind their neighbours in the exercise of severity in their eastern possessions, where their peculiar interest or policy required it. In the immediate neighbourhood of the waggon-road leading into town, the sad and melancholy spectacle may be daily witnessed of the mouldering bodies of poor black wretches, hung up *in terrorem* to the travellers to and from the country. In a conspicuous part of the town the gibbet is erected, and those other engines of torture that were frequently recurred to as a punishment previous to the arrival of the English. The unhappy wretch about to be launched into eternity, was broken upon the wheel, but those horrid cruelties have been now laid aside. Do we find from the history of mankind, that in employing those engines of torture, the prevention of crimes, (which ought to be the scope and end of all punishment) is more fully attained? There has hardly ever been an instance of the public execution of a colonist! That the white and black man should suffer the same punishment for the self-same crime, would be deemed by the Dutch

Dutch at the Cape a political abuse, tending to defeat the ends of justice. Riches can palliate crimes of the deepest dye, and purchase respect to the perpetrator.

Perhaps, in few European settlements, do slaves sell so high. They constitute, in fact, the support of the family to which they belong. From the sweat of their brow, gold is distilled into the pockets of their master; and from the easy manner in which many of the Cape residents are subsisted, we may in some degree account for the inactivity and indolence that pervade the whole. The labors of the slave, being thus a source of wealth to the family, we may naturally conclude that every care is taken of his existence. When a fit of sickness seizes the slave, the whole house become alarmed;— if he dies, tears are shed, not for the mere death of the unhappy wretch, but for the loss of the *rix-dollars* which they derived from his labor. So strongly is this idea of property rooted in the master, that the slave is not allowed to possess the common feelings of his nature. It is from the observance of little traits of character, which, by the bye,

bye, come not amiss to the pen of a gleaner, that we are enabled to form correct conclusions on the subject. Having one day visited a planter in the neighbourhood of our camp, I went to see a hyena, that had been caught the preceding night in one of those snares of which I gave you some description in a former letter. A slave boy, who had been more forward than the rest in teazing the poor animal, and who, from boldness in approaching him, had been somewhat in danger, was immediately sent away by one of the family with the following consolatory reprimand, delivered in all the guttural vehemence of the language in which he spoke, —' *Was he aware, that if he chanced to be torn in pieces by the hyena, that his master would sustain the irreparable loss of five hundred rix dollars?*' Whether a sense of danger, or the above sound reasoning, was of greater use, I cannot venture to say; however, the forwardness of the slave boy received a complete check. In this manner does the powerful voice of self-interest sweep, like the head-long torrent, every thing before it.

May

May the genius of philanthropy ever attend my friend; and may the warm effusions of disinterested friendship wipe from his bosom every anxious care that dares to invade it.   In the mean time,

                                        Adieu.

LETTER X.

Further remarks on slavery---The origin of this great evil con-
sidered---Slavery, as it existed among the ancients---Formerly
the punishment of crimes---The consequence of insolvency---
Wives and children frequently sold in the latter case---The
arbitrary power which the chief of a family possessed over
his children and slaves---Parents selling their children, another ground of slavery among the ancients---This unnatural custom expressly forbidden by the Mosaical law.

THE unfortunate class of mankind, who,
by *Christians,* are doomed to perpetual
slavery, is in general disregarded by the
observers of men and manners, and not
considered worthy the attention of the sons
of ease and affluence, to whom fortune,
or rather Providence, has been more favorable.

We

We are all too prone to look slightly over those evils which we do not ourselves endure, but which, nevertheless, sit not the more lightly on the wretched sufferers. It is only the benevolent heart that can feel another's woe—that can resolve to investigate the scenes of human misery, and contemplate the afflictions of his fellow-mortals with an eye of commiseration—that can ever let the scenes of slavery attract his attention. For my own part, I did not think the task which your benevolent curiosity imposed upon me, so irksome as I have on experience found it, nor once considered what melancholy emotions would arise in my own mind on contemplating the misfortunes of suffering humanity.

I have, however, undertaken a task which my own heart would not have permitted me to avoid, even if I had not bound myself by promise to my friend, and, in the course of my occasional remarks, have, in a loose and desultory manner, communicated in my two last letters the observations and reflections which my own feelings have prompted me to make on the evils

evils which Europe has, for her own interest, entailed on the hapless sons of Africa. I was in hopes that more agreeable scenes, and observations of a more pleasing nature, would soon have furnished something amusing for my epistolary correspondence, but an unexpected interval of inaction and leisure, has at present prevented me from visiting the dispersed farms of this extensive colony, and of entertaining you with an account of my gleanings in the interior of southern Africa.

This moment of leisure I have employed in extending my observations and reflections on the unhappy system of slavery, which has so long and so extensively prevailed, and been productive of such an accumulated mass of evils to mankind. I have not in this investigation relied solely on my own observations, and my own judgment, but have occasionally consulted the best authors who have treated on the subject. With many of these I know you are not unacquainted, but perhaps they have not made so lively an impression on your mind, as they have on mine, while

every

every day affords me an opportunity of seeing the verification of their recitals, and the justness of their remarks. I know your feeling heart will accompany your friend in tracing the origin, the causes, and consequences of one of the greatest evils exhibited in the moral system ; and if the dreary and disgusting view excite in your breast some melancholy sensations, they will be dispelled, and your mind will be exhilarated by the pleasing prospect that slavery must be gradually approaching towards its extinction.

The vast theatre of the moral world does not, among all its diversified scenes, exhibit a more disgusting spectacle than the existence of slavery, that odious and detestable system, which gives to one man so undue and unnatural a power over another. Equality among men is a chimera formed in the imagination of enthusiastic reformers; an ideal thing pleasing in an abstract theory, but incompatible with the plan of Divine Providence in the constitution of the moral system. In their origin, it is true, all men are equal, but in their

powers,

powers, natural as well as acquired, they are very unequal, and Nature has varied their talents as much as fortune, or rather Providence has diversified their condition. Some men are as evidently born to govern, as others to obey. Due subordination must, therefore, be maintained between the governors and the governed, otherwise the bonds of civil society will be relaxed, and no numerous community can long subsist in tranquillity. This is the chain which links together all civilized society, and is the foundation and support of all rational liberty. Slavery, on the contrary, that odious and abominable system, which renders one man the property of another, is the degradation of humanity, and a direct violation of the laws of Nature.

To bring forward to distinct inspection, the circumstances of that system, as it has existed among the ancients and moderns; to trace its history; to examine the principles on which it has been founded and carried on; to develop its causes, and display its effects; to endeavour to demonstrate the expediency and practicability of its abolition,

is

is my peculiar aim at present. In the course of the investigation, a comparison will be made between a state of slavery, as it existed among the ancients, and the modern system of negro slavery.

Slavery has existed in one part of the world or another, in every age since the time when men first began to be collected in numbers, and regular communities were formed. It is well known that it existed among the Egyptians, the Babylonians, the Jews, the Greeks, and the Romans, and there is little room to doubt of its prevalence among all other nations of antiquity.

The circumstances from which it originated, and the principles on which it was founded, were different. Sometimes slavery was the punishment of crimes, as it is now, in some instances, among most nations; but with this difference, that in the modern nations (of Europe at least,) delinquents condemned to slavery are employed in the service of the state, and commonly for a limited time; whereas, among the ancients, they were generally sold to individuals, either

either natives or foreigners. This kind of slavery has been sanctioned by most legislators, and, in its principle, does not appear unjust; at least, in civilized nations, where criminals have the privilege of a legal trial; and such a mode of punishment, properly regulated, may have a salutary influence on the morals of those who have rendered themselves obnoxious to it, and prove ultimately beneficial to the state.

Another principle of slavery was, the consequence of insolvency. The debtor who was unable to satisfy the legal demands of his creditor, was generally condemned to be his slave, and to satisfy, as much as lay in his power, pecuniary claims by personal services. This law admitted of different modifications and regulations at different times, and in different countries. Sometimes the debtor himself only, and sometims his wife and children along with him were delivered up to slavery; sometimes, also, they were sold with him in cases of criminal delinquency. This kind of procedure involving the innocent in the same punishment with the guilty, was diametrically

metrically opposite to every principle of justice and reason, and was founded on a very erroneous principle of ancient jurisprudence, which considered a man's wives and children as a part of his property, and equally so as his cattle. In the ages of remote antiquity, in most countries the chief of a family possessed the power of life and death over his children, as well as over his slaves. The laws established by Romulus, immediately after the building of Rome, gave to every father the absolute power of life and death over his children, and this exorbitant authority of parents continued some ages among the Romans; the father could put his children to death, sell them into slavery, or punish them as he pleased. The laws could not call him to any account on that subject. The same principle prevailed in some degree among the Jews; the authority of parents over their children was very great, but it was placed under legal restrictions. They did not, in their private capacity, possess the power of being the arbitrators of life and death to their children; and could only exercise it over such as were

refractory

refractory and disobedient by an accusation and proof before the magistrates, and in virtue of a judicial sentence pronounced by them.

Another ground of slavery among the ancients, was the custom of parents selling their children, which proceeded from the same erroneous principle of jurisprudence, and the same exorbitant power of parents over their children already mentioned, an unnatural authority, which existed in most of the nations of antiquity, and even at this day in some uncivilized countries; an authority so inimical to society, and so pregnant with mischievous consequences, that if its operations were not incessantly counteracted by parental affection, might be extremely prejudicial to a nation, and eventually cause its depopulation and ruin. Indeed, we may suppose, that nothing but a presumption that parental tenderness would prevent any abuse of this power, could have induced the legislators of anti-quity to leave it so long in the hands of parents. These laws and customs, however, although they long remained in force in different nations, have been gradually ex-ploded

ploded by the progress of civilization and religion, and are no longer found, except in countries not yet emerged from barbarism. It is not unworthy of remark, that this unnatural custom of selling children, never existed among the Jews, but was expressly forbidden by the Mosaical law, which prohibited the sale of an Hebrew to any foreign nation, and even limited to the year of release the servitude of those, who by reason of insolvency, became slaves to their creditors.

Amidst the dreary prospects of slavery, those historical remarks, besides illustrating the subject, and exhibiting a more extensive view of the circumstances with which it has been at different times connected, will tend to dissipate the gloom with which the mind of my friend will be liable to be overcast in contemplating those scenes of human misery.

Adieu.

LETTER XI.

The history of slavery continued—The capture of prisoners, its chief origin—Treatment of slaves in ancient times.

I AGAIN resume my pen to excite the benevolent emotions of the feeling mind of my friend. Your historical knowledge will enable you to accompany me in developing a far more fertile source, and more extensive system of slavery among the ancients, than that which arose from the sale of innocent children, and the punishment of insolvency. The reflections it will excite, cannot but be of a melancholy nature; but, while they rouse the feeling heart to commiseration, they inspire us with sentiments of gratitude to that Divine Providence, which

which has fixed our lot in a land of freedom, under the fostering influence of the
British constitution.

The causes enumerated in my last letter,
all contributed, in a greater or less degree,
to the introduction and continuance of
slavery among the ancients; but the principal and most productive source of that
greatest as well as most unnatural of human
evils, was the capture of prisoners in time
of war. The mode of carrying on war
among the ancients, was cruel and sanguinary. When a war was terminated by
treaty, we seldom find any provision made
for the ransom or exchange of prisoners in
the primitive times. During a series of
ages, the Romans were so far from ransoming their prisoners, that every Roman who
was so unfortunate as to fall into the hands of
the enemy, was esteemed legally dead, and
his property passed to his heir at law; and it
was not until some centuries after the building of Rome, that a law was passed to allow
the ransoming a Roman prisoner. In the ancient wars, when a province or country was
conquered without treaty or capitulation, the
                                        conqueror

conqueror imposed such conditions as he thought proper, sometimes pecuniary tributes, sometimes personal services by levies of workmen in rotation. In these particulars, different conquerors adopted different modes of acting, according to their political plans, and the nature of existing circumstances. The Jewish annals afford a long detail of their manner of treating their enemies. It was not their custom to make many prisoners. Under the conduct of Joshua, and other chiefs, they carried on their wars against the nations of Canaan, upon the principle of total extermination; and, in regard to other nations, it was their maxim to make captives only of the young women and children, and to put to the sword the married women, and all the males taken in battle, or in towns carried by assault.

In process of time, however, when the Israelitish monarchy was sufficiently established under the prosperous rein and vigorous administration of David, so as not to be in danger from any insurrection of the
subdued

subdued Canaanites, this exterminatory principle of warfare was, except in some instances, in a great measure laid aside, and
the remnant of the subdued natives of
Canaan, were suffered to live on condition
of paying tribute, and furnishing levies for
the public works, as they did for the temple,
and other magnificent structures erected by
Solomon. This was generally the mode of
treating the conquered among all the ancient nations; but the condition of those
people, thus reduced to a state of national
servitude, was widely different from that of
prisoners taken in battle, and in towns
stormed and sacked by the armies, who
were generally either put to the sword by
military law, or else sold into slavery, unless
the conqueror, for political reasons, thought
proper to dispose of them in some other
way, as it sometimes happened to be the
case.

Very little is known in regard to the particular modes of treating slaves in the times
of remote antiquity. Among the Greeks,
slaves were exceedingly numerous, and
often

often very hardly treated. Mr. Gibbon makes, in this respect, an observation which seems contradictory to reason, but is unfortunately verified by experience, that in those states where the subject enjoys the greatest share of liberty, the system of slavery has been carried to the greatest extent, and that slaves have been there treated with the greatest severity. Although the truth of this observation be exemplified and corroborated by the conduct of the Greeks and Romans, yet this conduct could not be an effect of the liberal system of their governments, but must have proceeded from some other causes.

It is, however, from the histories of Greece and Rome, that we learn the vast extent to which this odious system was carried, the principles upon which it was founded, the means by which it was supported, the extreme rigour with which it was at first exercised, its gradual relaxation, and the circumstances which led to its final abolition in Europe.

We must, from more modern records, and

and a new order of things, trace its origin and progress in America. My friend will accompany me in taking the melancholy retrospect.

Adieu.

LETTER XII.

Number of slaves in the Roman empire---Their immense number accounted for---Their cruel treatment during the first ages of the Republic---Their situation ameliorated by the progress of civilization and the introduction of luxury.

THE number of the slaves in the Roman empire is computed by Mr. Gibbon, an historian whose keen penetration, accuracy, and indefatigable industry, authorises us to believe that he has carefully investigated those matters, to have amounted to no less than one half of the inhabitants of the whole empire; and as the Roman empire is, according to the most moderate calculation, supposed not to have contained less than one hundred and twenty millions of people, the number of slaves could not amount to

less

less than sixty millions, a fact which strikes humanity with horror, and exhibits a dreadful and affecting display of the tyranny of man over his fellow mortals. This astonishing multitude of unhappy beings, of unfortunate rational creatures excluded from the privileges of society, and deprived of the common rights of mankind, consisted principally of prisoners taken in war, and their posterity; for, although some few had been purchased from foreign countries, the general mass of Roman slaves were persons of the former description.

The Romans, during the whole period of the existence of their republican government, were almost continually engaged in hostilities with the neighbouring nations. That military republic, intent on war, on rapine, and on conquest, allowing her citizens no repose, was incessantly directing her arm against the neighbouring states; every victory added fresh numbers to the daily increasing multitudes of Roman slaves; and as slavery was always entailed from generation to generation, if we consider the increasing posterity of the slaves, and the augmentation

augmentation of their numbers by the daily accession of prisoners taken in war, we shall not wonder at the amazing number of slaves in the Roman empire.

During the first ages of the republic, this unfortunate class of people were treated with extreme severity. Totally excluded from the protection and benefit of the laws, they were liable to the most rigorous punishment. The state, apprehensive of their numbers, and considering their desperate situation, enacted severe and sanguinary laws against them for the most trivial crimes; and, indeed, the Roman government could not use too much precaution against so numerous a body of men, so hardly treated, so daring, and so desperate. Those fierce and warlike barbarians, reduced from a state of military independence and warlike depredation, to a life of drudging and laborious servitude, were always suspected as dangerous to the state, and sometimes were actually found to be so. On this consideration they were put under the most severe and strict regulations, and their slightest irregularities punished with extreme and merciless severity;—besides,

sides, by the regulations of the state, every master, in his private capacity, had the absolute power of life and death over his own slaves. This absolute power of the master continued in force until the reign of the emperor Adrian, who deprived him of this unreasonable authority, and put the slave under the protection of the laws about A. D. 120, and 872 years after the building of Rome.

But, although the laws had not, during so long a space of time, done any thing in favor of that unfortunate class of men, the progress of civilization, and the introduction of luxury, had operated an important change in the circumstances of their condition; and instead of being constantly occupied in the most laborious drudgery, great numbers of them were employed in the houses of the wealthy citizens as domestics, agents, and ministers of luxury.

As I shall seize the earliest opportunity of resuming this interesting subject, for the present I shall bid my friend adieu.

LETTER XIII.

Historical remarks continued, setting forth the improved condition of the Roman slaves---The grand source of slavery exhausted---Their sufferings mitigated by the introduction of Christianity---Slavery in Rome abolished by the Gothic conquests---Feudal system of slavery established by the northern nations---Overthrown by the extension of commerce---Some traces thereof in Poland and Russia---Slavery introduced in the east---Prisoners of war made slaves by both parties in the time of the Crusades.

THE prospect begins somewhat to brighten, and we have a flattering view of the ameliorated condition of the slaves of ancient Rome. Every circumstance which exhibits any alleviation of human misery, gives pleasing sensations to the feeling heart, and will, I am sure, have the happiest effects on the mind of my friend. I think that I see his

countenance

countenance exhilarated in contemplating
the improved condition of the Roman slaves,
and his joy still increased in reflecting on
what the illustrious senate of Great Britain
has already done towards alleviating the
evils of modern slavery. It is a pleasing
reflection that the history of slavery, horrid
as it is to read, admits of some pages less
gloomy than the rest, and especially that
the British parliament, by its humane regulations, has so eminently contributed to
brighten the volume. We have now a
more pleasing retrospect of the gradual
amelioration of slavery; and a prospect still
more agreeable opens before us, which leads
us to expect, at a due time, its total extinction. I shall endeavour to entertain you for
a few moments with a continuation of my
historical remarks.

After the reign of the emperor Adrian,
the laws were more and more favorable to
the slaves, as were also the manners and
feelings of the people, as well as the general
circumstances of the empire. From the very
first establishment of the imperial government, the emperors had cultivated a more
pacific

pacific system than the republic had ever aimed at; and, as the wars became less frequent, more humanely conducted, and of shorter duration, with much longer intervals of peace under the imperial than under the republican system, the grand source of slavery was in a great measure exhausted. The natural consequence of this change was, that the numerous mass of slaves in the empire not receiving constant supplies, as before, by the capture of prisoners, the life of a slave was esteemed of greater value, and his person in every respect considered of greater importance. That numerous body of men did not then consist so much of captives taken in war, as of the posterity of those who had undergone that fate, and these being domesticated among the Romans, had acquired more peaceable and regular habits. Not retaining the indignant resentment, nor inheriting the fierce and ungovernable dispositions of their ancestors, they were become faithful servants. Thus, by a concurrence of various circumstances, the system of slavery was gradually softened, and the condition of slaves exceedingly meliorated.

rated. The gradual introduction of Christianity among the Romans, and at last its establishment in the reign of Constantine, before the middle of the third century, had also a powerful operation in favor of that unhappy and oppressed part of mankind. Indeed no true Christian, although he might chastise his slaves for their faults, could ever treat them with capricious and unprovoked cruelty. However, notwithstanding the happy effects of Christianity, and the favorable operation of other circumstances, a mitigated system of slavery still continued in the Roman empire till the Goths, and other northern nations, by a long continued succession of the most bloody and destructive wars that ever desolated and depopulated Europe, at length totally subverted the colossal power of the Roman empire, and overwhelming all in one general conquest, confounded every distinction. We are not acquainted with all the particular circumstances relative to these matters, but from a general view it appears, that these Gothic conquests, although destructive to the arts and sciences, to literature and civilization, had

had yet, among all the evils they produced, at least this good effect, of contributing to the abolition of that odious system of slavery which had so long existed, and prevailed to such an extent among the ancients, especially the Romans; but these northern nations, instead of the old, established a new, though less rigorous system of slavery, known by the denomination of the feudal system, which, by leaving an exorbitant power in the hands of the nobles, reduced the commons to a state little better than downright slavery. The nobles, taking advantage of every commotion, in process of time increased their power so much in many parts of Europe, as to set their sovereigns at defiance, and to reduce the whole mass of the people to the most abject state of villainage :—thus, instead of reposing under the guardian care of the magistrate, the people were deprived of the protection of the laws, and the nobles disdaining their authority, trusted solely to arms. This is a shocking picture of the state of society during the period alluded to; but such it was, and such it continued until the progress of civilization, and the

extension

extension of commerce, concurred gradually
to weaken, and finally to overthrow this
system of government, or rather of anarchy,
by giving wealth and importance to the
commons, and inspiring the nobles with
moderation and humanity. These favorable
circumstances were carefully attended to by
the princes of Europe, who let slip no opportunity of depressing the power of the nobles
and raising that of the commons, for it may
beobserved that a monarchical government
properly regulated, is of all others the most
attentive to the rights of the subject, and
the most favorable to the lower ranks of the
people. This great undertaking, the destruction of the feudal system, was at length
accomplished by granting charters to corpo-
rate bodies, and various other measures, but
above all, by granting permission to the
nobles to sell, and to the commons to purchase land, which proved a measure in
reality advantageous, and in most countries
agreeable to both parties, as the increase of
commerce, and the introduction of luxury,
had thrown considerable wealth into the
hands of the commons, and the nobles by
having

having the privilege of selling their lands, and also by enfranchising their vassals, and converting personal service, and rents in kind, into stipulated payments in money, were enabled to live more comfortably.

There are now but few traces of the feudal system remaining in Europe, except in Poland and Russia: indeed, it never rose to a more exorbitant height in any country than in Poland; but at this time many of the Polish nobles, impressed with sentiments of humanity, and a knowledge of their true interests, have enfranchised their vassals, and have found the measure equally conducive to the happiness of the peasants, and to their own advantage, by improving the cultivation, and augmenting the annual value of their estates: and the sovereigns of Russia (especially the late illustrious empress, Catharine) have, by many prudent regulations, begun to bring about the emancipation of the peasantry of that extensive empire.

The west had not emerged from the confusion into which it had been thrown by the subversion

subversion of the Roman power, when the east was astonished by the appearance of a new political and religious phenomenon, Mahomet and his successors. The Calyphs shook the eastern, or Constantinopolitan empire, to its centre; conquered Persia, Egypt, and the other northern parts of Africa, the kingdom of Spain, and several of the islands in the Mediterranean. It does not, however, appear, that those conquerors imitated the Romans in making slaves of their prisoners. The terms they offered to Christians were conversion to Mahometanism, tribute, or death by martial law. To Pagans they offered no other conditions than conversion or the sword, without leaving them the alternative of tribute; but, after the extinction of the Caliphate, the nations who founded their greatness upon its ruins, especially the Turks, adopted in its fullest extent the custom of making slaves of prisoners of war. The Christians in the time of the crusades retaliated, by adopting the same system, and inhumanity and enthusiasm on both sides, produced new scenes of horror.

In

In the laws of Godfrey of Bouillion, king of Jerusalem, in the commencement of the eleventh century, twelve oxen, or three slaves, were deemed an equivalent for one war horse;—thus, we see, a man was valued at no more than a third part of the price of a horse. At this time, the Turks are become more civilized, and conduct their wars generally on the same principles as the nations of Christendom, and the barbarous practice of making slaves of prisoners is chiefly confined to the Algerines, and other piratical states of Barbary. Slavery, however, is not yet abolished among the Turks, the Persians, and some other nations of Asia; but they content themselves with purchasing slaves, mostly children, from Georgia, Circassia, and other countries, where parents still possess the unjust power, and retain the unnatural practice of selling them.

Having thus exhibited a general view of this unnatural tyranny of man over man, and traced as concisely as possible its origin and causes, with the circumstances of its existence among the ancients at different periods of time, we are now brought to contemplate

template that train of events, that coinci-
dence of circumstances, and series of causes,
which gave rise to the system of negro
slavery. Here I shall at present bid my
friend adieu.

LETTER XIV.

History of modern slavery---Discovery of the new world by Columbus---Hispaniola, Cuba, Peru, Mexico, &c. conquered ---The natives reduced to slavery---Their miserable condition ---Benevolent efforts of the Bishop of Burgos, Father Bartholomew de las Casas, &c. in their favor---Contentions agitate the court of Spain and the Council of the Indies---Divers regulations adopted---The Americans in the Spanish settlements enjoy greater happiness at present than when first discovered by the Spaniards.

IT is now, my friend, that we are to begin to contemplate the system that so exceedingly disfigures the picture of the modern world. I have hitherto entertained you with a view of the system of slavery among the ancients; how happy should I be if I could here finish my details; how happy would it be for mankind, if the history of slavery

slavery could here terminate; but, alas! the blackest volume yet remains. The perusal of it will undoubtedly be a melancholy employment for my friend; but let us not shrink from the contemplation of human misery; the more attentively it is viewed, the more likely it is to be alleviated; it is too slightly observed, and too superficially considered. The tales of woe of which the history of slavery is composed are not pleasing to the philanthropic ear; but they make impressions on the benevolent heart which are often productive of the happiest effects. Let us then, my friend, resume our historical observations. The contemplation of causes and effects will in some measure amuse us in viewing a picture, on which the eye cannot look without horror.

Europe had, after a succession of almost ten centuries, at length emerged from that state of barbarism and anarchy into which she had been plunged by the subversion of the Roman empire, and the wars and revolutions which took place among the northern conquerors. After that universal wreck of the arts and sciences, and of every species

species of literature, commerce and civilization making a gradual progress, had concurred to effect the revival of learning and the arts, and the governments of Europe had acquired stability and permanency. The world thus began to assume a new aspect, and a new order of things had just taken place, when Christopher Columbus projected the most adventurous and daring enterprize that ever entered into the mind of man, and, by discovering a new continent, introduced upon the theatre of the world a train of events equally novel and interesting, and still operating with undiminished activity upon the political and commercial interests of mankind. Populous cities are now seen in the immeasurable wildernesses of America, and commercial towns on her formerly unknown and uncultivated shores. The discovery of America has effected a most important change in the aspect of the world, and the condition of mankind. This interesting event, by pouring into the old continent a continual supply of gold and silver, has extended the commerce, and caused more than a sixfold advance in the value

value of the landed property and produce of
Europe; and has unfortunately carried into
the inmost recesses of Africa scenes of horror before unknown among her uncivilized
inhabitants.

Immediately after the return of Columbus
from that important expedition, daring adventurers, followed by bands of unprincipled
desperadoes from Spain, daily poured into
the new world. Hispaniola, Cuba, and
other islands were conquered; settlements
were made on the terra firma, and the isthmus of Darien, and finally Peru and Mexico were subdued, the former by Francis
Pizarro, and the latter by Ferdinando Cor-
tez, after a series of hardships and adven-
tures, of exploits and successes unexampled
in the annals of history. These adventurers,
thirsting after the riches which the new world
offered to their avarice, soon discovered their
own small numbers to be inadequate to the
cultivation of the soil, and the working of
the mines, even had they been inclined to
labor; but that was entirely contrary to their
dispositions and turn of mind, for all those
who at that time emigrated from Europe
to

to the new world, went with a view to obtain riches by conquest and rapine, and not by the slower means of patient and persevering labor. These unprincipled and inhuman invaders, thus circumstanced, reduced the unfortunate natives to the most distressing state of slavery. They parcelled the land among themselves, and with the lands the unfortunate inhabitants also, every one, according to his dignity and office, having a certain portion of lands, with a proportionate number of inhabitants assigned to him. These ill-fated slaves were compelled not only to cultivate the lands for their imperious masters, but also to work in the mines, a species of labor with which they were entirely unacquainted; indeed, the natives of those countries were but little inured to labor, and from their habits of life totally averse to and unfit for it. Accustomed from their infancy to a hot and enervating climate, the strength of their bodies was not adequate to the exertions of long continued and toilsome labor. They scarcely used any clothing, and lived on the simplest food, a small quantity sufficing them; the fertility

of

of the soil, aided by the continual heat of
the climate, produced spontaneously almost
as much as was necessary for their support.
Men, accustomed to such a mode of living,
were absolutely incapable of supporting the
hardships imposed upon them by their unfeeling masters. Death, the only consolation, and last refuge of the unhappy slave,
gave to multitudes that repose which they
could not hope ever to enjoy in this life,
and Hispaniola and other islands were almost entirely depopulated before the justice
of the court of Spain had the opportunity
of exerting itself in favor of this oppressed
people. Whoever would desire to know the
detail of these barbarities, may, if his feelings will suffer him to peruse the shocking
recital, read the relations of the bishop of
Burgos, father Bartholomew de las Casas,
and other humane Spaniards, both laymen
and ecclesiastics, friends of humanity, and
advocates for their oppressed fellow-creatures, who spared no pains in exposing these
enormities to the eyes of Europe, in order
to excite sensations of pity, and rouse the
justice of the courts of Spain and Rome in
favor

favor of the oppressed natives of America. In process of time their benevolent efforts produced a good part of their desired effects, although every species of opposition was exerted against them by the colonists. During the whole reign of Charles V., those contentions between the friends of humanity in Spain, and the interested pro- prietors of the colonies, (of which I shall speak more fully in my next,) continued to agitate the court of Spain and the council of the Indies. The public voice of human- ity had generally the ascendency; divers regulations were successively adopted, and all of them in some degree favorable to the natives of America. At this time the Ame- ricans in the Spanish settlements are far from being in a distressed condition. They cannot but now enjoy a greater share of political and social happiness than when the Spaniards found them. The Americans, or as they are frequently called the Indians, in Mexico, Peru, and the other colonies, lead at present a civilized life, profess the Christ- ian religion, possess lands, and live in vil- lages governed by their own caciques; and

are

are only as tributary people, obliged to pay certain taxes to the Spanish government, and to submit to certain regulations imposed upon them by their conquerors, of which the most menial is that of being obliged to work in the mines. All the Indians in Mexico and Peru, and the other countries where the mining business is carried on, are obliged to work in the mines by rotation six months in the year, if they live within thirty miles of any mine that is opened, and this service they perform by levies in rotation eighteen days at a time, for which they receive wages to the amount of 2s. 3d. sterling per day. In a general view, we must grant that the natives of America enjoy a greater share of happiness under the Spanish government than they ever did under their own despotic and tyrannical rulers, which no one can doubt of, who for a moment reflects on the superstitious and sanguinary system of the Mexican religion, and the multitude of human sacrifices annually offered to their deities in Mexico.

It is now time to suffer my friend to withdraw himself from the contemplation of a picture

picture which has already filled his mind
with melancholy reflections on the depravity
of the human heart; and if I cannot promise any thing of a more exhilarating nature
in my next epistle, a little repose may, however, enable him the better to sustain the
shock which a view of those horrid scenes
is apt to give.   I shall therefore, at present,
bid an affectionate farewel.

LETTER XVI.

The cruelties exercised upon the hapless natives of America, reported to the court of Spain by Bartholomew de las Casas --Contentions between the colonists, and the friends of humanity---The courts of Spain and Rome take them under their protection---Report of the colonists respecting their aversion to labor, which is accounted for---Negro slavery unfortunately suggested by de las Casas, through motives of humanity---The manner the negroes were seduced---Zeal for religion concurred to promote this measure---The minister Ximenes reluctantly consents to the plan of negro slavery, proposed for the emancipation of the Americans---A trade to Africa for slaves consequently commenced by the Spaniards, and soon adopted by all those nations which had established colonies in America.

I AGAIN resume my pen, in order to present once more to my friend's contemplation, scenes of horror and human depravity. You will, I know, accompany me (not cheerfully, indeed, but feelingly) in in those melancholy walks, and enjoy, at least, the benevolent emotions of your own philanthropic mind. Our ability to relieve misfortune, and lend a supporting hand to indigence and distress, may be circumscribed by various causes, but to wish well to all mankind is a pleasure of which no earthly power or circumstances can deprive the benevolent heart, and this pleasure, I know, my friend enjoys in its fullest extent. It will, therefore, be no small source of satisfaction to reflect, that, in the midst of those horrid scenes, some illustrious characters were found who excited all their powers to alleviate the sufferings of their fellow mortals.

Among the friends of humanity who exerted themselves to procure the emancipation of the hapless natives of America from the tyranny of their merciless oppressors, the name of Bartholomew de las Casas stands in the most eminent place. He had been an eye-witness of the cruelties exercised by the colonists upon the unhappy victims of their insatiable avarice, and these cruelties he had constantly condemned and resolutely

resolutely opposed. He carried an exact account of those proceedings to the court of Spain, and endeavoured to excite the public voice of compassion throughout the whole kingdom.

From Spain he applied to Rome : he laid the affair before the sovereign pontiff in order to rouse the thunders of the church against the colonists. The colonists, on their side, by their agents both in Spain and at Rome, were always ready to counteract his benevolent efforts. They represented the natives of America as creatures of an inferior nature, absolutely incapable of being instructed in the Christian religion, and those who had embraced it, were excluded from the sacraments, and other privileges of Christianity. The friends of humanity applied to Rome in behalf of these ill-treated people. At length the courts of Rome and Spain took them under their protection, and rendered them more tranquil, as I observed in my former letter.

The colonists then represented the Indians to the court of Spain, as a people so totally averse to labour, that no rewards—no wages

wages could induce them to work, and that nothing but absolute compulsion could oblige them to put their hands to any sort of useful employment. In this they certainly said no more than the real truth : unaccustomed to the conveniences and luxuries of a civilized life, they were also unacquainted with its wants. They contented themselves with little food, and that of the simplest kind, and the constant heat of the climate precluded the necessity of clothing. As for gold and silver, they had no use for those metals. In such a state of society, indolent leisure, and the liberty of roving about at pleasure, constituted the supreme felicity of the natives of the greatest part of Spanish America, consequently the expectation of wages and reward had no influence over them. They esteemed it madness to confine themselves to daily labour, for what they could do so well without, and could not imagine what motive could induce the Spaniards either to labour themselves, or desire others to labour for the acquisition of things not necessary for their subsistence. This indolent disposition of the natives, if complied

complied with, was represented by the colonists as totally subversive of every prospect of national advantage, which might have been expected from the discovery of the new world. They represented to the court of Spain, that as no rewards whatever could induce the natives to leave off their indolent mode of living, and apply to useful labour, the settlements could not be cultivated, nor the mines wrought, without making use of compulsory means.

This argument involving considerations of national advantage, proved an insurmountable obstacle to the success of those who pleaded the cause of the Indians. But Las Casas, determined to carry his point, cast his eyes on every side in order to discover the means of accomplishing his darling object—the exemption of the Americans from slavery; and most certainly, without foreseeing the consequences, unfortunately hit upon a plan which has been productive of an aggregate of evils—a series of calamities to which the history of the world scarcely affords any parallel.

This humane and benevolent man, with the

the most philanthropic intentions, by a fatal mistake, and without being able to foresee the extent to which such a measure would be carried, and the miseries it would produce, conceived the plan of negro slavery.

The Portuguese, under the conduct of Vasco di Gama, had sailed round the Cape of Good Hope to India, A. D. 1494, only two years after the discovery of America, and in coasting round Africa in this and some preceding voyages of discovery, had become acquainted with the negroes.

Happy had it been for that unfortunate people, had they to this day remained as ignorant of the Europeans as they had ever been before that period. Like the simple natives of America they gazed with admiration on the ships as well as on the complexion of the strangers thus come to visit them, little apprehending what a load of calamities they were about to heap upon them and their posterity. Las Casas, revolving in his mind the means of emancipating the natives of America imposed upon them by the colonists, and finding this impossible to be accomplished, unless other hands could be procured to work the mines, and cultivate the plantations, turned his eyes towards Africa. He considered the negroes were a strong-bodied race of men, whose muscular and firmly-compacted frames, rendered them much more capable of enduring fatigue, than the natives of America. He observed, also, that the negroes were not so averse to labour as the Americans. On these considerations he imagined, that if slaves could be procured from Africa, they would be far more useful, and would be able to support those fatigues which threatened no less than the total extirpation of the whole race of the Americans, whose bodies were utterly inadequate to such exertions.

Zeal for religion, also, concurred to promote the measure. He made no doubt of the conversion of the Americans when once exempted from slavery and oppression, in which case they would leave a numerous posterity of sincere Christians, who, adopting the habits of civilized life, would become good subjects, and useful members of society; whereas, the labors imposed upon them

them could ultimately have no other effect than the total extermination of their race, and the consequent depopulation of the colonies. He supposed, likewise, and with reason, that the introduction of negroes into the colonies, would prove a great accession to their population, and to the increase of their produce, by such an additional number of useful hands.

In these circumstances of the infant colonies, the measure, though harsh, might be necessary, and if provision had been made for the emancipation and establishment of the negroes after a limited time of servitude, might have been very advantageous to the newly-discovered countries, without being prejudicial to the cause of humanity; although, even in this case, how strongly soever necessity, or the prospect of national advantage might have apologized for the adoption of the project of negro slavery, and however beneficial the measure might ultimately have proved, the effects could not have justified the means used to produce them. No man can have a right, in any case, to use compulsion towards another, but by legal

legal means, and upon legal principles. It would be unjust to rob one man in order to enable us to relieve the wants of another ; and it could not be just to force the Africans into slavery, for the purpose of relieving the Americans. Perhaps Las Casas, seeing no other alternative but the introduction of African or the continuation of American slavery, thought the toleration of a less evil, in order to eradicate this greater, a necessary and excusable expedient. This active ecclesiastic submitted his plan to the consideration of Cardinal Ximenes, who was then at the head of affairs in Spain, and was himself a zealous advocate for the emancipation of the Americans from the tyranny of their oppressors. This minister at first rejected, but at length very reluctantly gave his approbation to the measure.

The Spaniards opened a trade to Africa for slaves, and the slave-trade thus commenced by Spain was soon adopted by all those nations which had established colonies in America and its dependent islands, and has been since carried on to such an extent, and

and accompanied with circumstances so shocking to humanity, that it may justly be considered as one of the greatest evils that ever existed in the world---an aggregate of the greatest calamities ever inflicted upon any part of the human species!

I must now for a while leave my friend to the melancholy contemplation of those scenes of horror which the avarice of Europe has produced in the unoffending regions of Africa and America. In these disquisitions my friend will readily perceive, that I am supported by the authority of M. L'Abbé Raynal, and that celebrated historian, Dr. Robertson, besides many others of distinguished reputation.

I shall now proceed to the reflections which have been the result of those enquiries, and lay them before my friend, little doubting of his entire approbation, and as little of his firm persuasion that with unfeigned respect and esteem,

I am, &c.

LETTER XVI.

Reflections on the negro slavery---Comparison between a slave among Christians, and a slave among the pagans of ancient Rome---The case of the former proved more unjust and severe---Roman slaves were esteemed in proportion to their talents---Instructed in Greek, Latin, &c.---They were not ill treated, nor employed in drudgery---Rome proved to have been particularly favorable to slaves.

I NOW proceed, according to my intention and promise, to lay before my friend a series of reflections, the result of my historical enquiries relative to a system that has been in all ages so conspicuous a blemish in the picture of the moral world.

Having, as concisely as possible, displayed the origin of slavery, and the barbarous principles upon which that unnatural tyranny of one part of the human species over

over another was founded, with its different modes of existence, at different periods and in different countries, from its first establishment among the ancients, to the present iniquitous and inhuman system of African slavery among the moderns, let us, in the next place, proceed to examine, by the principles of sound reason, without passion or prejudice, the condition of the enslaved African, to make an estimate of his calamity, and compare his afflictions and the evils he suffers among Christians, (the professed disciples of the meek and merciful Jesus) with the condition of a slave among the pagans of ancient Rome.

If we compare the condition of the enslaved negro, with that of the captive taken in war, the cases are in no respect parallel. The calamity of the latter, and the hardships of his fate, bear no proportion to the misery and the injuries suffered by the former. According to the barbarous mode of making war in ancient times, the life of an enemy taken in arms was forfeited by martial law, consequently, when made a prisoner, his person was entirely at the disposal

posal of the conqueror, who, according to
the sanguinary maxims of ancient warfare,
might, if he pleased, immediately take
away his life, which was forfeited by the
law of arms.   If the enemy spared his life,
it was purely an act of clemency, and he
had an undoubted right to impose upon him
what conditions soever he pleased.   Therefore, according to the ancient martial law,
if he made him his slave, there was no injustice in the case.   This the slave very well
knew, and if he was used with any degree
of lenity, he had no reason to complain of
his destiny, conscious that his treatment was
no worse, but perhaps much better than
that which his master would have met with,
if the fortune of war had put him into his
hands.   According to the established maxims of the times, he had no right to expect
better treatment.   Whoever lifts his hand
against another, ought not to murmur when
he feels the blow returned.   Whoever makes
war his profession, ought to be contented to
abide by the chance of war, and to be pre-
pared to meet defeat and captivity, as well
as victory and triumphs.

   This right of the victor over the vanquished,

quished, extended also to their posterity; for he who permitted his vanquished enemy to live and beget children, possessed the same right of property in the children, as in the parent; and thus slavery was perpetuated, being entailed and transmitted from generation to generation. Neither had the descendants any right to complain, if treated with humanity; for they owed their all, their very existence to the clemency of the enemy, who had spared the life of the parent, without which act of mercy his descendants had never existed.

All this is strictly just according to the principles of pagan morality, and a necessary consequence of the sanguinary maxims of ancient warfare. The case of the unhappy African is, in every point of view, entirely different. The unoffending negro, in the forests and morasses of Africa, never so much as meditated hostility against Europe. He never gave any offence---never offered any injury to those who came from a distant quarter of the globe to make a prey of his person, as the wolf makes his prey of the lamb. From the peaceful retreats of his native country---from his paternal fields, he

is

is, by barbarous tyrants and inhuman men-stealers, dragged to the sea coast, and delivered up to irremediable and hopeless slavery. His condition is also different from that of the Roman slave in many other respects: he is purchased for the sole purpose of being employed in the most laborious drudgery—the case was not so with the Roman slave. The slaves of Rome, in the first ages of the Republic, it is true, were hardly treated; but after Rome had acquired the sovereignty of all the countries around, annihilated the rival state of Carthage, and conquered the western parts of Asia, luxury rushed in like a torrent, and the citizens of Rome lived in all the pomp and splendor of Asiatic magnificence. Those who are conversant in the history of the Romans, and acquainted with their manners, are not ignorant that luxury, parade, and every kind of expensive magnificence, were never carried to such a height in any city, ancient or modern, as in Rome. That city, which had employed more than seven hundred years in plundering the world, had concentrated within her walls the spoils of
the

the vanquished nations, from the Euphrates to the Atlantic ocean, and from the Danube to Mount Atlas in Africa, and many of the Roman citizens exceeded sovereign princes in opulence and grandeur.

Ammianus Marcellinus, a native, and during a great part of his life an inhabitant of Rome, gives a striking description of the luxury and splendid mode of living which prevailed in that immense city, forty years after Constantine had removed the imperial residence from Rome to Constantinople, a period in which Rome, by losing the presence of the court, and being no longer the seat of government, may reasonably be supposed to have somewhat declined from its former grandeur.

All these circumstances were exceedingly favorable to the condition of slavery, for, as I have already stated in a former letter, an almost incredible number of slaves were employed in the houses of the wealthy citizens in the capacity of household domestics.

Many of the physicians of Rome were slaves, as were, also, many of the teachers

of

of grammar and rhetoric, of the languages and mathematics, so that the condition of the slaves at that time at Rome, was less unhappy than it has, perhaps, ever been in any other part of the world. The person of an useful slave was considered of great importance, and he was esteemed in proportion to his talents. T. Pomponius Atticus, was a great dealer in slaves, as, also, was M. Crassus, and many others. Atticus took care to bestow a good education on those who shewed marks of genius. He instructed them himself in the Greek and Latin languages, as well as in logic and rhetoric, and carefully superintended every part of their education. A learned slave was often sold for several hundred pounds sterling. This plainly shews the esteem and consideration in which valuable slaves were held by the opulent Romans, and at the same time affords a convincing proof that slaves so highly estimated, would not be ill-treated, nor employed in mean drudgery. These circumstances are not to be wondered at, if we take a view of the manners and customs of the Romans, and of their mode

of

of living both at Rome and in other parts of the empire, in the latter times of the republic, and afterwards under the imperial government.

The state of society among the Romans, was widely different from that which prevails among the nations of modern Europe. The Romans, even under their emperors, although they had lost their fierce republican spirit, still retained a veneration for the forms and modes of the commonwealth. The emperors themselves, at least such of them as knew and consulted their true interests, affected the same veneration for those ancient forms and nominal distinctions.

The most tyrannical and most daring of them never durst assume the title of king, contenting themselves with that of imperator, which we translate emperor, a word which, in the modern languages, is used to express the greatest extent of regal power; but the word imperator, among the Romans, was entirely a military title, and signified no more than generalissimo, or commander-in-chief of the armed force of the

the republic, and had been given to several generals in the purest ages of the republic; the republican dignities of consul, tribune, censor, pontiff, &c. still continued, which Augustus had the address to unite in his own person, an artifice very commonly made use of by the succeeding emperors, so that the Roman empire might, with propriety, be defined an absolute monarchy under the form of a republic---a proof how much mankind are influenced by forms, and governed by names!

The Romans, who almost to a man would have revolted against the best regulated and best administered regal government, could tamely submit to one more despotic than any monarchy in Europe, contenting themselves with retaining some empty and useless republican names and forms; and they, who would have massacred the best of their rulers if he had dared to assume the title of king, could patiently suffer every species of oppression under the most sanguinary tyrants, invested with the title of imperator, or emperor. These republican ideas had a very great influence

ence on the state of society, and modes of
life among the Romans. Scarcely any Roman citizen would, for the sake of gain,
so far debase himself as to become a menial
servant in the family of another of his fel-
low-citizens; nor were there many citizens,
how poor soever they might be, who were
necessitated to embrace such a situation for
the sake of procuring a livelihood.

The conquered countries were obliged to
pay an annual tribute to Rome, part in
money and part in their respective produce.
The Roman citizens were thus supplied with
all the necessaries, and most of the conveniences of life. Egypt and Sicily were the
granaries of the republic, and supplied
Rome with grain; some countries furnished
wine, some oil, some cattle, &c., and a
daily distribution of these things was made
to such of the Roman citizens as had a legal
claim to it. At first those distributions were
made monthly, weekly, or at other stated
periods. Afterwards, in order to indulge, and
retain in a state of tranquillity a proud, lazy,
improvident and restless people, public
ovens were built, and the Roman citizens
being

being furnished each one with a ticket,
came and received daily donations of money
and bread, as also of wine, oil, bacon, and
other articles, so that the poorer class of
Roman citizens being by such privileges almost entirely exempted from the necessity
of working, few of them would submit to
a state of servitude for wages, like the
lower class of subjects in modern Europe.
No state of society could have been more
favorable to the Roman slaves.

In the palaces of the grandees of Rome,
all the domestics, the agents and ministers
of luxury and parade, as before remarked,
were of that description. The household
even of the emperor himself was mostly
composed of slaves. In modern Europe
the various offices of the sovereign's household are esteemed the highest honours, and
are usually conferred on the higher class of
subjects; but among the Romans, those
offices were generally filled by slaves: so
different are the modes of society and national manners in different countries and at
different periods of time. The same system of society prevailed in all the other
cities

cities of the empire, each of which was an epitome of the metropolis.

Another custom extremely favorable to slaves became also very prevalent in the Roman empire, especially in the capital. The opulent and powerful citizens some-times from motives of gratitude, often of vanity, enfranchised their slaves in reward of their fidelity, and zeal in their service; and as a slave had no country of his own, by the laws of Rome he became, when enfranchised, a citizen of that country to which his master belonged. Thus the powerful citizens of Rome attached to themselves a numerous body of freemen, who still continued, from motives of gratitude and interest, to look up to their former masters as their patrons and protectors. This practice became so common in the latter times of the republic, that the state thought it necessary to enact laws to restrain it, and to exclude those enfranchised slaves and their descendants for three or four generations from the public offices of the commonwealth. These laws and regulations, however, in process of time, became obsolete. Slaves and their descendants,

descendants, by enrolling themselves in the armies in times of public danger, and by various other means, often arose to high promotion.

All these circumstances held out promising expectations to the slaves of ancient Rome. Every one who possessed any considerable talents, had the greatest reason to form the most sanguine hopes not only of freedom, which, under the imperial government he could always obtain by enrolment, but also of high advancement. This was the most powerful antidote against the evils of slavery that could possibly enter into that condition. Hope is in every situation of difficulty and danger, the firmest support of the mind—it softens every toil, and sweetens all the ills that are incident to life. It is the pleasing expectation of once again seeing my country and my friend, that cheers my spirits at the southermost promontory of the old continent,—that gives animation to my mind and pen,—causes me cheerfully to communicate my reflections, and bid my friend, for the present,

Adieu.

LETTER XVII.

The hopeless situation of the enslaved African---His condition more deplorable than the Roman slave---That of the slaves among the Turks, Persians, &c. far preferable---Of the slaves, male and female, in Turkey---Their condition different from that of the negro slaves---The erroneous opinion of their being naturally devoid of sensibility---Their feelings are lively, and their attachments strong---The Hottentots and Laplanders afford incontrovertible proof---Mr. Park's observations alluded to---Our knowledge of the interior of Africa very imperfect---The difficulties which travellers have encountered---Further allusions to Mr. Park---The lower class of people not so unhappy under the feudal system of government as generally supposed---This confirmed by the observations of M. de Reisbeck and Mr. Cox.

I ENDED my last epistle with pleasing reflections on the animating nature of hope, that greatest of cordials, and I commence the present with the same subject in view. I had observed the delightful, and not improbable

probable expectations of freedom and promotion which might sweeten the bitter cup
of slavery in the latter ages of Rome. Such
favorable circumstances, such flattering prospects, such opportunities of acquiring ease,
comfort, and promotion, do not present
themselves to the enslaved African. In such
a situation, pleasing hopes, although never
realized, might at least console the hours of
adversity, and cheer his mind with agreeable ideas; but such is not his case. To
him even the faint solace of illusive hope is
in a great measure wanting. Condemned
to toil and labor in order to enrich others,
slender are his hopes, and few and hardly
earned his opportunities of procuring freedom and comfort.

Thus, after an impartial examination of
the circumstances of the prisoner taken in
war, and carried into Roman slavery, and
those of the peaceable and unoffending
African forcibly torn from his native home,
the cases appear in no respect parrallel; let
us consider the situation of the slaves purchased in foreign countries. Among the
Romans, the number of these was small, but,
among

among the Turks, and other nations where slavery still continues, that is now the common method of procuring them. If we compare the condition of the slaves thus procured among the Turks, the Persians, &c. with that of the African slaves in the colonies, we shall find the former in general far preferable. The slaves thus purchased by those Mahometan nations are disposed of among the great men; and a very considerable part of them are purchased by the government, and rise to great promotion, many of them being advanced to the highest offices and honors. The Mamalukes, a military corps composed of those slaves, seized on Egypt about A.D. 1250, and the Mamaluke kingdom of Egypt continued until A. D. 1517, when it was conquered by Sultan Selim II. In Turkey, at this day, the celebrated corps of Janissaries and Spahis consists of slaves thus purchased from foreign countries, chiefly Circassia, Mingrelia, Georgia, and the neighbouring parts; for they cannot procure slaves from Mahometan countries, it being expressly prohibited by the Koran to enslave or retain in slavery

slavery any person professing the Mahometan religion; so that as soon as these slaves thus purchased are initiated in the faith of the Koran, which all those purchased by the government immediately are, they are esteemed freemen, although there is no real freedom in those countries. The seraglios and harams consist of female slaves thus procured; and the great officers of state are chosen from among the males. Both the political and military administration of the Turkish empire is, for the most part, exercised by persons originally slaves, purchased from Christian parents of the lowest class. This may be esteemed a phenomenon in the history of government. Such men, under no other control than that of the Grand Seignor, have the whole legislative and executive power entrusted to their hands: but, not to enter farther into these details, we may observe one very important circumstance which interestingly discriminates the condition of the negro slaves from those purchased by the Turks and other Mahometans.

The

The slaves purchased by the Turks and Persians are generally children. Their habits of life are not formed; social connections have not fixed their attachment to their native country. After the first tears shed at leaving their parents and their native land, they retain but little remembrance of, or affection for either; to their unnatural parents surely no affection is due. They look up to their master as their only parent and protector. The case is far different with the enslaved negro.

The unhappy African is torn from his native country after his habits are formed, and a thousand ties fix his attachment to the country where he first saw the light. Some have persuaded themselves, and endeavoured to persuade others, that the negroes are a stupid race, and that their natural insensibility, together with the uncivilized state of society in which they have lived, prevents them from having the nice feelings of the civilized nations of Europe, or even of Asia. This opinion, although adopted by many persons, is very erroneous, equally contrary to reason and experience,

rience, and which nothing but an absolute
ignorance of human nature could either produce or excuse. The affections of the mind
are natural, not acquired. Learning, civilization, philosophy, and the various improvements of the human mind, regulate, but do
not strengthen those feelings; they have, on
the contrary, rather a tendency to diminish
their force. The unlettered milk-maid will
be as deeply affected at parting from a
favorite lover as the daughter of a noble-
man; and the mud-walled cottage exhibits
as striking instances of parental, filial, and
conjugal affection, as the palaces of the rich
and great. History affords numberless examples of persons in exalted stations and
refined manners, who have set at nought
those tender feelings, which scarcely any
consideration could tempt the lower classes
of mankind to violate. Polished life, or an
extensive and varied conversation with the
world, quickens and improves the intellectual powers, but deadens the feelings. The
affections of the mind are observed to ope-
rate the most powerfully in those countries,
where the state of society approaches the
nearest

nearest to a state of nature. This has been sufficiently observed among the savage tribes of North America, and other uncivilized countries. The feelings of savages are exceedingly strong, their attachments are unalterable, and their enmities implacable. They are firmly attached to their parents, their friends, and their country. Of this the Hottentots and the Laplanders afford an incontrovertible and striking proof. The Dutch at the Cape settlement have not, until lately, been able by any enticement, indulgences, or rewards, to prevail on any of the Hottentots to domiciliate themselves in that place, and comform to the European manner of living; although many attempts had often been made, and all possible means tried for that purpose. It is likewise a fact well known, that Laplanders have been brought to Copenhagen, and although accommodated with every thing that could gratify desire, and supplied with every luxury the metropolis of Denmark could furnish, yet they could never reconcile themselves to polished life, but continually sighed after their former endearments among the snowy

snowy mountains and dreary morasses of their dear native country.

It is clearly proved from a number of instances, that a Hottentot, or a Laplander, is as strongly attached to his country as ever was a Greek or Roman patriot; and there is no reason to doubt, but the uncivilized African in his reed-thatched hut on the banks of the Niger, has as lively feelings, and as strong an attachment to his family, his friends, and his native soil, as the polished European in his elegant villa on the banks of the Thames, the Tagus, or the Seine.

Perhaps some who have perused the most authentic information we have been able to procure concerning the interior of Africa, may imagine that they see reason to treat what is here said as empty declamation, and an exaggerated statement of the case. Alas! it is easy to treat as trifles those calamities we do not feel, but the unhappy objects on whom they are inflicted ought to determine the point; let those who feel them say, whether they be trifling or serious evils. It may, indeed, be alleged that the greatest part of the slaves brought from Africa, far from

from being injuriously deprived of freedom,
were never in possession of that inestimable
blessing, but were slaves from their birth,
and never knew any other state than that of
servitude. This must be granted; it is certainly too true. That intrepid and intelligent traveller, Mr. Park, informs us, that
three-fourths, at least, of the inhabitants of
Africa are in a state of slavery, and that in
their wars, the far greatest part of the prisoners who are sold to the slave-traders are
always of that class, a circumstance for which
he assigns very substantial reasons. Of those
who take the field, he says, the greatest
number are always slaves, who are compelled to attend their masters, consequently
the greatest number of the prisoners, if it
be for that sole reason, must generally consist of persons of that description. These
slaves also being obliged to fight on foot, or,
if sometimes on horseback, being much
worse mounted than those of free condition,
are consequently less capable of making
their escape in case of a defeat. The same
gentleman asserts, that in the coffles of slaves
brought from the interior, he always found
                                       that

that a very small proportion of them had ever been in a state of freedom.

The relations of Mr. Park, as far as they go, have every appearance of truth. No one at least will deny them the merit of probability. He certainly made use of the best means in his power to procure correct information, and having exerted great talents and industry in acquiring a knowledge of the Mandingo language, found better opportunities of obtaining such information than could have been expected: but it is impossible to obtain a complete knowledge of all the particulars requisite for forming an accurate judgment on these matters, without a long residence in the country; consequently the shortness of Mr. Park's stay, the distressing circumstances of his journey, the continual fatigues he underwent, and his frequent want of the necessaries of life, as they proved insurmountable obstacles to his proceeding as far as Tombuctoo, the place of his destination, so they could not fail of preventing him from making such accurate observations, and from obtaining such correct information of distinct particulars as his abilities would

would in more favorable circumstances have enabled him, and his zeal have prompted him to procure.

After all, the interior of Africa is, in great measure, *terra incognita* to the Europeans. Circumstanced as those remote regions are, both in a physical and moral view, the information we can obtain of their inhabitants and their police is as vague and imperfect as our knowledge of their geography. Few attempts have been made to explore those vast regions, and these have been attended with little success. The persons who have undertaken the task have experienced such hardships, and met with such disasters, as are sufficient to deter others from imitating their example, and reiterating the attempt. The difficulties which Mr. Bruce encountered in the eastern part of that continent, the unfortunate death of Mr. Ledyard, the deplorable catastrophe of Major Houghton, and the hardships and dangers to which Mr. Park was incessantly exposed, will deter every one from following their footsteps who is not endued with courage equal to theirs. The last-mentioned gentleman advanced

vanced some days journey beyond Sego,
the capital of Bambarra, and nearly reached
the extremity of that negro kingdom, having
penetrated 800 miles east from the factory
of Pisania, and about 1120 miles east from
the promontory of Cape Verd; but being
prevented from proceeding further by a
combination of difficulties and distresses,
which no human fortitude or perseverance
could surmount, he returned to Pisania by
a quite different route from that by which
he set out. The active abilities and persevering courage displayed by Mr. Park in
this arduous undertaking, command our admiration and challenge our applause; for,
although his tour bears but a small proportion to the extent of that continent, few persons have contributed more to the improvement of the interior geography of Africa, or
collected more important information relative to African police, and the system of
society among the negro nations.

In regard to what that enterprising traveller says concerning the system of slavery
universally established in Africa, to enter
into minute details would exceed the limits
of

of a letter. It is, however, necessary to observe in general terms, that he describes it
as nearly resembling the feudal system formerly existing in this and other countries of
Europe, and the condition of the African
slaves as not differing much from that of the
villains in the feudal times. Now, if we
make a just estimate of the case, according
to our uniform experience of the nature and
conformation of the human mind, we shall
find that the lower class of people were not
so unhappy under the feudal system of government, as we in this age of liberty, and
in the present more improved, civilized, and
enlightened state of society are apt to imagine. Habit had reconciled them to the
system under which they lived; they entertained no hopes of enjoying a greater liberty; their ideas were contracted within their
own sphere of life; their minds were not
exercised in the contemplation of a state of
freedom; they were attached to their native
soil; they were easy and comfortable in
their family connections. The very same
picture of human life is at this time exhibited
in those countries where the feudal system
yet

yet prevails, or has lately prevailed. That system was not abolished in Bohemia before A. D. 1781, nor in Hungary until A. D. 1785, and in Poland and Russia it still exists. Those travellers, however, who visited Hungary and Bohemia previous to the emancipation of their peasantry, never observed any particular marks of infelicity in the countenance or behaviour of that class of people. M. de Reisbeck, and our countryman Mr. Cox, two very intelligent travellers, whose accuracy of observation, and judicious mode of estimating men and things, entitle them to every degree of attention and regard, although they cannot avoid both observing and lamenting the unhappy state of the inferior classes of the people in those countries in comparison of their situation in countries where a greater degree of freedom exists, yet they do not seem ever to have discovered that those people felt themselves so unhappy as it might be supposed. M. de Reisbeck has sufficiently expatiated on the general state of Hungary and Bohemia, but cannot refrain from remarking the gay and cheerful

disposition,

disposition, and apparent contentment of the half-naked populace in those countries: and not only Mr. Cox, but all the travellers who have visited Russia, have remarked the cheerfulness and hilarity of temper which so strongly characterize the very lowest class of the people in that country. They are habituated to their condition; they have been fixed in it from the age of infancy; they see it the same as that of the greatest part of their neighbours, and neither amuse nor torment themselves with distant comparisons. If this was the case of the enslaved Africans, their lot would be less pitiable, and would not have excited the compassion of so many eminent philanthropists, nor should I have so long employed my pen in delineating their condition, in order to display it to the view of my friend, to whom, for the present, I beg leave to bid a short farewel.

LETTER XVIII.

Reflections on the state of society---The ideas of people assimilated to their station---The negro, though in a state of bondage in his own country, must be feelingly affected at being
sold into European slavery---Arguments in favor of this observation.

IN resuming my pen I purpose to submit
to your consideration some reflections which
may be made on the state of society, perhaps, in every country, and which arise
from circumstances that highly merit the
attention of the judicious observer of men
and manners. It is evident that happiness
and misery depend in a great measure on
the opinions entertained in the mind, and
human opinions arise from human circumstances. He would have but a small claim
to the title of a moral philosopher, who
should be ignorant that two different persons

sons might be placed in the same situation of life, in which, while one of them would find his happiness as complete as he could wish, the other would be completely miserable. The richest clothing, or the daintiest fare, would not constitute the happiness of a parent forcibly torn from his children, or of an affectionate wife compulsively separated from her husband. The feelings of the heart are the criterion of happiness or misery.

In the most refined and civilized countries, even where the greatest degree of freedom prevails, and is enjoyed by every class of the inhabitants, there may always be found a number of individuals, whose condition is in effect little better than that of a slave, yet habit renders such situations, if not pleasant, at least tolerable. The laboring man, oppressed by the burden of a numerous family, and obliged to work as hard as slaves, perhaps, any where do, with scarcely ever a moment of leisure, sees notwithstanding, without the least envy or discontent, the splendid palace, the abode of opulence and luxury arise in the vicinity of

his

his homely hut.   He cheerfully employs
his hours in labor.   His ideas are assimilated
to his station.   His hopes and expectations,
from the first dawn of reason, never flattered him with the prospect of a much
happier lot. The poorest day-laborer would,
notwithstanding, be as sensibly affected at
being torn from his family, his connections,
and his native soil, and sold into foreign
slavery, as the high-spirited man of fortune.
The Russian peasant has as great an aversion against being torn from his home, and
forcibly enrolled in the army, as any free-
born Englishman could have; and although
military or naval service in Russia confers
freedom, it is well known that volunteers
are more difficult to procure in that country
than in England or France; and, whatever
we may think of the matter, our forefathers
under the feudal bondage would have felt
the same sentiments of horror at the apprehension of being sold into foreign slavery,
as an Englishman of the present age. Reasoning from the justest analogy, founded on
the immutable principles of human nature,
we may therefore with certainty conclude,
                                         that

that a negro, although in a state of bondage
in his own country, is as feelingly affected
at being sold into European slavery, as an
Englishman would be at becoming a slave
to the Moors or Algerines. Happiness and
misery are in a great measure dependant
on a certain association of ideas, and their
limits are determined rather by the imagination than by any external circumstances.
From this cause it proceeds that a degree
of felicity is sometimes found in the humble
cottage, which is not to be met with in the
lofty palace. The greatest luxury which
opulence can procure is not sufficient to
confer happiness. Crowns and sceptres
sometimes cannot give it, and all the combined efforts of ambition and avarice cannot
obtain it. If we investigate the cause of this
phenomenon, why happiness is often absent
from the mind to which power, opulence,
bodily health and vigor, and all the whole
train of temporal blessings and advantages
combine to give it an easy entrance, we
must direct our observations to the invariable principles and universal feelings of
human nature. Some imaginary want is
                                perceived,

perceived, some ideal disappointment is supposed to be met with, something, in fine, which causes the mind to fall short of that happiness of which it had formed a distant and illusive prospect. The cause of that contentment and cheerfulness of mind so often conspicuous among the very lowest orders of the people, must be traced to the same source, to the feelings, the predilections, the attachments of the mind, the force of habit, and the assimilation of their ideas to their situation. A person may form a just estimate of what a poor African must feel at being for ever separated from all he held dear, by imagining himself placed in his situation. To render the human mind for ever miserable, by doing violence to its feelings, is the extreme of cruelty. It is, as far as in us lies, an act of homicide committed on the soul of man; but ambition and avarice have at all times sported, not only with the interests, but the feelings of mankind. This shocking, but important reflection, I shall at present leave to the consideration of my friend. Adieu.

LETTER XIX.

Of the capture of Constantinople in 1454, when the citizens were carried into slavery---This similar to the case of the negroes---Their condition represented less deplorable by some, and perhaps exaggerated by others---The state of slavery in America varies in different places---In some it is more tolerable than in others---The negro slaves in Mexico far more comfortable than those elsewhere---Representations consequently partial, inaccurate, and contradictory---Conclusions must be drawn from leading facts and general observations---The evil consequences of the slave-trade illustrated by only one circumstance---The sufferings of the Africans incontrovertibly proved by their depopulation---Enquiries into this unparalleled destruction of the human species.

AN inhabitant of civilized Europe cannot read, without shuddering with horror, the melancholy account given by Phranza of the memorable capture of Constantinople by assault, A. D. 1454, when the persons, as well as the property of the inhabitants, were

were given up to the army by Sultan Mahomet II., in consequence of the rash courage
and obstinate valor of the Emperor Constantine Paleologus, who to the last refused
the most honorable and advantageous terms
of capitulation, and bravely fell in defend-
ing the breach through which the Turks
entered the city.   Phranza, who being one
of the principal officers of the court of Constantinople, was an eye-witness of the whole,
and himself a sufferer in the general calamity, relates that the citizens, without any
distinction of age, sex, or rank, were dragged
from their hiding places, especially from the
church of St. Sophia, into which vast numbers had crowded, and being chained together like beasts, were driven through the
streets, and carried into slavery.   The imagination may conceive some kind of general
idea of the horrid scene, but it is impossible
to describe the feelings of the unhappy victims.   My friend is ready to say within
himself, " how shocking would such a spectacle appear in any European city with
which we are acquainted;" and if we were
in Africa, and should see the bands of
negroes

negroes collected from different quarters of the interior by merciless tyrants; husbands torn from their wives, and wives from their husbands; parents from their children, and children from their parents; and all promiscuously delivered up to the slave-merchants, who string them together like horses, and then conduct them to the sea-coast; if we should see all this, could the imagination of man paint a scene of greater horror? What arrows of heart-rending anguish must transpierce the soul of an unfortunate African thus torn from his native country, from his paternal home, from all his endearments, from every object of his affection, and carried into perpetual and irremediable slavery! What powers of eloquence can express, or what vigor of imagination conceive the soul-rending reflections which must torture an unfortunate wretch in whose breast are concentrated all the subjects of corroding grief that can prey upon the mind? If we follow him to the plantations, will the picture exhibit more pleasing colors? Will his condition there afford a brighter, a more enlivening prospect? Can imperious commands,

toilsome

toilsome labor and coarse food, afford him any consolation, or make him forget his family, his friends, and his native country? or can the whip of the task-master extinguish reflection? Alas! it may banish it for a moment, but it will constantly return, and with redoubled force. Some, in their descriptions of negro slavery, through interested motives, or in consequence of superficial observation, represent the condition of slaves in the colonies as less deplorable than is generally imagined; while others, through an excess of humanity, may perhaps exaggerate, if it be possible to exaggerate, the evils they endure; and no doubt local circumstances may authorize different opinions in these particulars.

The state of slavery in America and its dependancies, as it is the case in every circumstance of human condition, varies in different places, and in respect of different individuals. In the Spanish settlements in Terra Firma, on the Rio de la Plata, but above all in Peru and Mexico, the condition of the negroes is considerably more tolerable than in the islands. Peru and Mexico being the

the source of wealth, and centre of luxury, dissipation, and indolence, a greater number of negroes are employed as domestics in those countries than in the islands; and the mines, as I mentioned in a former letter, being wrought by corvies of Indians, negroes are seldom employed in that laborious work. Both Mexico and Peru contain several great cities, where many of the inhabitants, both Spaniards and Creoles, live in a very luxurious manner, in regard to parade and ostentatious shew, which obliges them to keep a great number of domestics, who are mostly negroes, and lead a far more easy and comfortable life, than those who labor in the plantations. Of all the cities of the modern world, perhaps Mexico is that in which the inhabitants live in the most extravagant style of luxury, and ostentatious parade. This luxury, like that of ancient Rome, is a circumstance extremely favorable to the slaves, by causing them to be employed in the houses of the great and opulent, and to compose a great part of their retinue; and all the writers who treat of the European settlements, describe the condition

condition of the negro slaves in Mexico as far more comfortable than that of those in any other part of the new world.

In the examination of a system of so complicated a nature, and so extensive an operation, involving such a number of particulars, and subject to so many variations, owing to local and changeable circumstances, no just conclusions can be drawn from particular cases, the representations of which will always be partial, inaccurate, and contradictory.

In reasoning upon this, as upon every other circumstance of ancient or modern history, we must be contented to conclude from leading facts and observations of a general nature. Every situation of human life admits of unbounded variety, being influenced by a thousand external and adventitious circumstances impossible to enumerate, and scarcely any thing can happen so disastrous, as not to be ultimately beneficial to some. The greatest public calamities, even war, pestilence, famine, earthquakes, &c. redound to the profit of some individuals; but we ought not for that reason the
less

less to deprecate these destructive and cala-
mitous events; and if the state of slavery
has proved a fortunate circumstance to some
particular persons in that situation, it is no
argument in its favor, and can neither palliate the horrors of the system, nor justify
its existence.

Proceeding, therefore, upon general principles and general views, it will suffice to
instance only one circumstance of the slave-
trade, which sufficiently displays in the most
conspicuous and striking manner, the dreadful magnitude of the evil.   M. l'Abbé Raynal, an author of deserved celebrity, and
who possessed the most extensive means of
information, asserts, that since the commencement of the slave-trade, between eight
and nine millions of negroes have been imported into the colonies, and that notwithstanding so prodigious a number imported,
not more than one million and a half are
now to be found in all the European settlements!!!   If this calculation be not exceedingly exaggerated, it shews a destruction of
the human species to which the history of
mankind affords no parallel; and let this
question

question be put to every person who has the smallest feeling of humanity remaining in his breast, whether all the riches drawn from the new world can compensate for so horrid a massacre of his fellow-creatures; whether all the tobacco and coffee, all the rum and sugar, all the gold and silver ever brought from America and her islands, can balance so extensive a score of calamity? Every one, whose heart is not steeled against compassion, and callous to the sufferings of his fellow mortals, will have the answer ready; to hesitate would argue the total extinction of every sentiment of a rational being. Would it not have been a greater happiness to Europe never to have known the productions of the new continent, than to have thus added so black a volume to the long history of human misery?

This astonishing and unexampled destruction of the human species, is a proof more convincing than a volume of particular facts and insulated arguments could afford, of the hardships endured by those poor Africans, and at once confutes all that can be alleged concerning the lenity of their treatment;

ment; and, as it is an instance of depopulation unparalleled in the annals of the world, it is equally curious and interesting to inquire into its causes. That celebrated and philosophical historian, Dr. Robertson, expatiates at large on the causes of that depopulation which ensued among the natives of America, in consequence of the slavery to which they were reduced by the first Spanish adventurers. He represents the natives as men of weak bodies, and unfit for labor; and says, that on any emergency, when the Spaniards were willing to exert themselves, one Spaniard was able to perform more laborious work than five or six Indians. This he ascribes to their indolent mode of living, which exempted them from using vigorous exertions, to the insipidity of their food, and the small quantities they were accustomed to take; for, although the Spaniards are the most abstemious people in Europe, yet it was observed, that if one Spaniard could undergo as much labor, he also required as much victuals as five or six Indians, and the natives were astonished at the quantity of food devoured by the Spaniards,

as

as well as at the quantity of work they were
able to perform.   From these physical principles Dr. Robertson very rationally con-
cludes, that men of so weak a frame, and
so little accustomed to laborious exertions,
were totally incapable of supporting the
toilsome drudgery and excessive labor imposed upon them by their conquerors, and
that consequently their feeble constitutions
sunk under the burden.   However, by the
account of the Spaniards themselves, the
Mexicans, although inhabitants of the torrid
zone, were not so very deficient in strength,
and much less in courage; but the disparity
was too great between an army of men,
though few in number, trained to European
tactics, and armed with European weapons,
and a multitudinous mass of unorganized
and undisciplined troops, armed with no
better weapons than pointed stakes or spears,
with heads made only of a sharp-edged flint,
or other stone, and in this seems to have
consisted the superiority of the Spaniards
over the Mexicans, as much as in their
superior strength or courage. Notwithstanding this remark, Dr. Robertson's mode of
reasoning,

reasoning, as far as it goes, is certainly just and appropriate; but he seems to have overlooked, or at least very slightly touched upon a cause of a moral nature, which perhaps operated as powerfully as any of the physical causes he enumerates, to the destruction of those unfortunate savages. This was that dejection of mind, that sinking of the spirits, which could not fail of being the natural and certain consequence of seeing themselves reduced from a state of comfortable ease and peaceful security to which they had ever been accustomed, to a state of slavery, toil, and drudgery under imperious and merciless task-masters. This dejection of mind, which must have overwhelmed their strength and spirits, may easily be conceived if we reflect on the circumstances of the case, and consider ourselves in their situation. If we contemplate in a parallel point of view the situation of the Spanish conquerors and that of the conquered and enslaved Indians, we shall see that no two situations in life could be more completely different. Their circumstances were diametrically opposite. The Spaniards
who

who made the first conquests and settlements in America, were men long accustomed to a naval and military life. Their bodies were inured to every kind of hardship, their constitutions seasoned to every climate and every mode of living, and their minds were formed for daring enterprizes. These desperate adventurers undertook those conquests at their own expence and risk, and receiving nothing but commissions from the court of Spain. They embarked their whole property, and all their credit, in these hazardous undertakings, and consequently had no alternative between exorbitant wealth and honor on the one hand, and extreme poverty and distress on the other. Their minds were intent on great acquisitions and brilliant achievements. Their heads were filled with romantic projects; their imaginations were continually fixed on great and daring enterprizes, and the hasty accumulation of riches. Their courage was buoyed up with expectation, and whatever they undertook, they were determined to carry their point. It is no wonder that such men, in such circumstances, with such ideas, and animated

animated with such prospects, should be capable of great exertions; but the condition of the poor, enslaved natives, formed the most striking, the most absolute contrast to that of the Spanish adventurers. Forcibly torn from all they valued or held dear, they saw themselves doomed to a life of toil and labor, without any cheering ray of hope, without any enlivening prospect. This could not fail to contribute as much as any of the physical causes which Dr. Robertson has mentioned, and perhaps more than all of them together, to debilitate those unhappy Indians, and hurry them in multitudes to the grave. The dejection of mind inseparable from such a situation could not fail to produce this effect. In all difficult, dangerous, or painful undertakings, the mind alone supports the man. This every one can ascertain who has investigated the nature of the human mind, and its influence over the bodily frame. Physicians well know that the affections and passions of the mind have a powerful effect on the body, and that the most vigorous constitution cannot long bear up under an extreme and

and continual depression of spirits, from whatever cause it may proceed : thus causes purely of a moral nature often have a physical operation, and the problem, arising from the astonishing and unexampled depopulation which has taken place among the Africans in the colonies, admits of an easy solution. The human species in every part of the globe multiplies, and becomes more numerous, unless it be diminished by war, pestilence, famine, emigration, or other adventitious causes. The negroes are as prolific in their own country as any other people; and it is the interest of the masters to encourage their propagation in the colonies. Some moral cause then must be assigned for that unparalleled waste of human life, which cannot be attributed to any causes of a nature purely physical. It cannot be attributed either to their labor or their food. The negroes are a strong-bodied race of men, well formed for labor, and not many are imported but such as are of a sound body, and of an age proper for supporting fatigue; nor can we suppose them ever to have been much accustomed

customed to dainty fare. Neither can it be attributed to the climate. Their native country is situated in the torrid zone, under the same parallels of latitude as the West Indies, and the air of Guinea is hotter, more suffocating and insalubrious, than in almost any part of the American world. This is an evident proof, among many others, that this horrible destruction of the human species does not proceed from any physical causes. The real cause of a circumstance so shocking to humanity, is therefore a subject of inquiry worthy the attention of the philosopher and the philanthropist. I beg leave to take an affectionate farewel.

LETTER XX.

The real cause of that havock which slavery has made among
the negroes---Their bitter anguish---Multiplied calamities---
The slave-trade incompatible with Christianity---Confutation
of the arguments in favor of it on the score of religion.

SINCE the amazing destruction of the
human race displayed in the case of the
unfortunate Africans, is not to be attributed
to any physical causes with which we are
acquainted, since their bodies are well formed for labor, and their former habits have
inured them to no very dainty fare, we
must look to the mind for the true cause of
this shocking phenomenon, which has never
been thus uniformly exhibited in any other
race of men. Yes, my friend, the mind is
the seat of happiness and of misery, and
here we can discover the real cause of that
havock

havock which slavery has made among the unfortunate Africans. The more we examine the matter, the greater reason we shall have to be confirmed in our opinion, and shall easily conceive the anguish of mind which they must suffer.

History commemorates the misfortunes of the great; romance delights to paint in glowing colors the fancied sufferings of imaginary heroes; and full-mouthed tragedy represents the calamities of illustrious personages, who have acted a conspicuous part in the theatre of the world; but if a circumstantial history of slavery could be written, every page, every paragraph would furnish a tragedy. Alas! of the history of slavery no more than some faint outlines can be given; but if all its horrid circumstances, all its shocking consequences could be related; if the imperious commands to which its unhappy victims have been obliged to submit, the unreasonable requisitions with which they have been forced to comply, the barbarous insults they have suffered, the corroding reflections, and heart-rending anguish that have embittered the lives of those
unfortunate

unfortunate wretches could be exhibited to public inspection, who could bear to contemplate such scenes? what eye could, without shedding a deluge of tears, peruse such annals of misery? and yet, in all this history of human woes, negro slavery would fill the blackest volume. If we trace the unfortunate negro from the moment he is forcibly dragged from his native country and paternal home, to the last moments of his miserable existence, if we could view his toilsome days, his sorrowful nights; if we could be acquainted with his melancholy reflections and the bitter anguish, that like a torrent must rush upon his soul at the remembrance of his lost liberty and former endearments, the most unfeeling would be moved with compassion, and interest itself would give way to humanity. In the negro slave we should see an unhappy being, on whose devoted head is accumulated the whole aggregate of wretchedness, the sum total of human misery; and is it possible that a rational being can contemplate such scenes of multiplied calamities, without sentiments of commiseration?

It

It is, indeed, difficult to conceive by what subtilty of logic the slave-trade can be proved compatible with the Christian religion, which teaches unlimited charity, universal benevolence, and by a direct and positive injunction from the mouth of its Divine Author, commands us to do to others as we would that they should do to us.

By some it has been alleged, that the slave-trade affords an opportunity of converting the Africans to the Christian faith. But what sort of Christians can this mode of conversion make? What opinion can a poor enslaved African have of the Christian religion, who every day of his miserable life has in his own person so fatal an experience of the cruelty of its professors? If Europe sincerely desires the conversion of Africa, she certainly makes use of very ill-contrived means, and employs very ill-chosen apostles. Others have endeavoured to justify negro-slavery on another ground. The interior of Africa, they say, is governed by savage despots, in a continual state of hostility with one another; numbers of prisoners are taken in those contests among the negro princes,

who

who would probably be massacred, if the Europeans did not afford them an opportunity of thus converting them into a profitable article of commerce. This may in part be true. We know but little of the inland parts of Africa, notwithstanding the enterprizing efforts of Mr. Park and others, as already observed; but this description is not much unlike the picture her interior regions may be supposed to exhibit. However, it is somewhat questionable whether so unhappy a state of society, if it really exists in Africa, can justify the slave-trade carried on upon her coasts. Reasoning from the most evident probabilities, and we have nothing else to reason from, our acquaintance with those regions not being sufficient to supply us with facts and observations, we cannot but suppose that this opportunity of making merchandize of their prisoners, is one of the strongest incitements to those destructive and savage wars among the negro chiefs. If none would buy none could sell; and it is a principle of jurisprudence as well as of sound reason universally known and acknowledged, that no one has a right to buy of of those who have no right to sell. It is likewise alleged in favor of the trade, that numbers of criminals are sold into slavery, who, if the Europeans did not purchase them, would suffer death as the punishment of their crimes. Such may be the case with some, but in such a state of society as exists in Negroland and Guinea, it is an easy thing to accuse and condemn an innocent person, the will of the chief is fully sufficient. In that country the accused can have no legal trial; his acquittal or condemnation rests in the sole disposal of despotic power, and what can be a greater temptation to the violent exercise of that power in criminal cases, than the prospect of making a profitable merchandize of the condemned? While the slave-trade is carried on by the Europeans, the arbitrary and unprincipled chiefs of Africa will never be at a loss to procure slaves, either among their own subjects by criminal condemnation, or among those of their neighbours by predatory hostilities.

In reasoning on this part of the subject, a circumstance of considerable importance ought not to pass unnoticed;—when crowds

of

of negroes are conducted to the sea-coast for sale, can the European traders hold a court of judicature, in order to ascertain the guilt of each individual, and to discriminate between the guilty and the innocent? Have they the means of inquiring into these matters among people of whose laws, customs, and language they have so little knowledge, and at the distance, perhaps, of several hundred miles from the place where the crime is alleged to have been committed? Under these circumstances it is easy to perceive that the European trader, were he ever so conscientiously disposed to make justice his guide, could not ascertain the criminality or innocence of the person exposed to sale; neither could the poor slave, however innocent, have the means of making his innocence appear.   For the present, my friend, adieu.

LETTER XXI.

Confutation of the arguments against the abolition of the slave-trade, on the score of national advantage.

IN my last I observed the principal arguments that can be adduced either in support of the system of negro slavery, or in favor of its abolition, when the subject is considered merely in a religious and moral point of view. If it be examined on the ground of expediency and national advantage, arguments of a weighty nature, and involving a variety of distinct and important considerations, may be brought forward on each side of the question. A most formidable phalanx of arguments are ranged in battalia against its abolition, arguments deduced from the nature of the climate, the dispositions of the negroes, and a variety of other

other circumstances. The impossibility of cultivating the plantations without slaves has long been asserted; and if this impossibility really exists, there is but a faint prospect of ever seeing slavery abolished in the colonies. This was the argument principally insisted on by the first Spanish colonists, to justify, or at least to excuse their tyranny over the native Americans; and this is the most preponderating argument in favor of the system of negro slavery at this day. But is this impossibility real or imaginary? Is it not possible to cultivate the plantations of tobacco, sugar, coffee, cotton, &c. in the colonies without slaves, as well as the corn-fields and vineyards of Europe? In all the European countries we see magnificent edifices erected, highways cast up, navigable canals cut through extensive tracts of country, in a word, the most stupendous monuments of human industry produced without the labor of slaves. We see not only agriculture, but an endless variety of the most difficult manufactures, brought to a very great degree of perfection, without the labor of slaves; and why the colonies could not be cultivated
without

without slaves, appears somewhat problematical. It is alleged that the sultry climate of those countries render it impossible that they should be cultivated by Europeans. Such an obstacle might indeed be insurmountable at the time of their first colonization, especially as the natives could not be prevailed on to work for wages; but there are now a sufficient number of negroes in those parts, who are accustomed both to the climate and the work, and also inured to labor. These men, if enfranchized, and animated by freedom and wages, would cultivate the soil; and living comfortably on the fruits of their industry, would propagate, and constantly keep up a race of robust laborers inured to the climate. Here, however, another obstacle occurs, and, as it arises from considerations of self-interest, the *primum mobile*, the main spring of human actions, it merits particular and attentive consideration.

If an abolition of the slave-trade, and the emancipation of the slaves, should take place, the negroes being no longer slaves but free-men, day-laborers, and commanding

ing wages in proportion to the quantity of work they perform, the cultivation of the plantations would be much more expensive, a circumstance of which the natural and inevitable consequence would be a considerable advance in the price of their productions, which would bear hard upon the consumer in Europe, and ultimately diminish the consumption of colonial produce.

That the abolition of negro slavery would enhance the prices of the different articles of colonial produce, is a position of which we must acknowledge the truth, and consider the consequences in the fullest extent of their operation on individual and national interest. Europe would pay dearer for the commodities imported from her colonies; but she would at the same time see a new channel opened for the exportation of her own produce and manufactures. The negroes would live in greater affluence, and consequently would have a greater demand for European merchandize. One negro family would then consume a greater quantity of European commodities than perhaps five, or perhaps than ten do at present; for

as

as money constantly circulates, there is no doubt but the negroes, like other men, would expend in proportion to their means of acquisition. This is an invariable effect of the natural disposition of mankind to enjoy the conveniences, and, perhaps we might add, the luxuries of life, as much as lies in their power; a disposition which is general in all nations, in all ages, and in all ranks of society, notwithstanding the seeming deviation of some eccentric or avaricious individuals. The emancipation, and the consequently increased affluence of the negroes, considered in this point of view, could not fail of being conducive to the extension of European commerce; for the industry of Europe will be excited, and her trade will flourish in proportion to the consumption of her colonies, if the assertion of M. l'Abbé Raynal be founded in truth, " that every settlement in the torrid zone requires the cultivation of a province in Europe, and that this is the real advantage which Europe derives from her colonies." This prospect of national advantage from the emancipation of the negroes, is highly deserving of the attention

attention of the European states, of Great Britain in particular, as being the principal commercial and manufacturing nation. In this I know your sentiments will coincide with mine.

I am, my dear friend,

Yours, &c.

LETTER XXII.

Continuation of the subject---The argument against the emancipation of slaves, for fear of their depredations, answered.---
A gradual liberation recommended---Those who have been
the longest in slavery, should be the soonest set free.---The
whole emancipation should be completed as soon as possible---
The troubles of St. Domingo are not a substantial argument
against negro emancipation.

IN resuming the argument, I must observe, that as to the objection, that the advanced prices of the articles of colonial
produce would diminish their consumption,
it requires but a small degree of reflection
to perceive, that this could be no more than
a momentary evil. The greatest probability
is, that such a consequence would be scarcely
perceptible. The colonial productions, esteemed at their first introduction as luxuries,
are

are now become necessaries of life to the inhabitants of Europe. Every one, in proportion to his means of gratification, uses as great a quantity of these commodities as he thinks requisite, and no more; and those who possess, in the very least degree, the means of indulgence, consume as great a quantity of them as they are able to procure. This is the case at present, and to all appearance ever will be so. The sugar, tobacco, &c. of the colonies, are now become as much the necessaries of life among all classes of people, as the butter and cheese of Europe.

If some retrenchment of those superfluities, should take place among a few individuals, it will probably be so small as to be scarcely perceptible in the general system of colonial traffic, and its transient effects will soon vanish. The causes which will augment the wealth and population of the colonies will produce a similar effect in Europe. In proportion as the wealth and population of Europe and her colonies increase, the reciprocal demand for each other's productions, will infallibly be increased; this is a natural

a natural and necessary consequence, so
that the very measure, which, on a superficial view, might seem calculated to cause
a decrease of the demand for colonial produce in Europe, will, upon mature consideration, appear to promise eventually a quite
opposite effect.

All the commodities of European produce or manufacture, are exceedingly increased in value within the last half century; so is the land which produces them,
and the labour employed in their produc-
tion, but the consumption of those articles
is not diminished. While wealth and population flourish, commerce will flourish
likewise, and buyers will be found. These
things have a reciprocal influence—they go
hand in hand.

As another argument against the abolition it is alledged, that the tranquillity of
the colonies would be exposed to imminent
danger, from the emancipation of so great a
number of slaves, who, being intoxicated
with the sudden acquisition of freedom,
might, perhaps, abandon themselves to a
life of licentiousness and depredation, instead

stead of adopting the peaceful habits of industry. This might be the case with some.
Such men there are in all countries—but
cannot laws and regulations be made to restrain them? Must we cut off the hand of
an honest man, to hinder him from becoming a thief? Or is it necessary to retain men
in slavery, through a surmise that they may
possibly make a bad use of liberty?—Far
be such maxims from the liberal mind!
Whenever the negroes shall be made free-
men, let such of them as make a bad use
of their freedom by any infringement of the
law, be punished according to their demerit.
Let a code of laws, calculated upon just
and liberal principles, be made for the colonies, and let every disturber of the public
peace, black or white, suffer condign punishment. There is no doubt but the negroes would, like other men, see and con-
sult their true interest, by preferring a life
of industry and peaceful security, to a life
of continual uncertainty and danger, and
regulate their conduct by the laws, as well
as the populace of the different countries of
Europe.

However

However, as it is always imprudent to risk the introduction of one evil, by the removal of another, it might possibly be improper to emancipate all the negroes at once. In that case, a certain number might be set free every year, or every six months; and those who had been the longest in slavery, ought to be the soonest liberated. But if such a regulation should take place, commissioners, of strict consciousness and humanity, should be appointed to superintend the business, to take care that the slaves suffer no ill-treatment during the remaining part of their servitude, and that it be not unjustly prolonged beyond the period fixed by the laws. This period ought to be as short as it could be deemed consistent with prudence, that so the whole emancipation might be completed as soon as possible, without endangering the tranquillity of the colonies. It would, indeed, be much better, if the whole business could with safety and propriety be completed at once, and every vestige of slavery be effaced at one stroke.

The troubles of St. Domingo, and the massacres

massacres there committed by the rebellious negroes, afford a plausible, but not a substantial argument against negro emancipation. The enormities committed in that once flourishing settlement, are not the necessary effects of that emancipation, but rather have originated in the circumstances of the times in which it took place. Such a state of things in both Hispaniola and Guadaloupe, is a natural consequence of that disorganizing system which, during a long time, convulsed the mother country as well as her colonies. Had the emancipation of the negroes been directed by the British government, or had that event taken place either under the former or present government of France, there is very little reason to think that the revolt of those islands would have taken place.

Under a peaceful and regular system, the enfranchised negroes would have become industrious cultivators of the soil, and useful members of society. Instead of this, the circumstances of the times were such as immediately obliged them to take up arms, and drew their attention from the dig and hoe, to the musket and bayonet. This was the fatal cause which produced such pernicious effects. Indeed, the conversion of a numerous body of abject, oppressed, illiterate and savage slaves into a military band, i n spiring them, at the same time, with the highest republican notion, and the most licentious ideas of equality, was too strange and too violent a metamorphosis, not to be attended with dangerous consequences.

This, however, I hope will never more be the case, and in this benevolent wish I know that you, my friend, sincerely join me, while, with esteem,

I am, &c.

LETTER XXIII.

The negroes, if emancipated, would be an useful class of sub-jects.---The colonies would make a rapid advancement in civilization and opulence.---It would benefit Europe.---The disturbances in the French settlements render the present movement not altogether proper for the immediate extension of freedom.---The objection that several colonists would lose considerable sums, by being deprived of the negroes they had purchased, might be removed by a subscription for that purpose at the expence of the state, or by a temporary tax---Cursory remarks on the first projectors of African slavery---The general aspect of the world, seems favorable to its abolition---The completion must be left to the wisdom of parliament---An address to the imperial senate on the subject---The British government has done more than any other in Europe towards the amelioration of the condition of the negroes---Affairs of magnitude require much serious consideration---Concluding reflections on the subject.

No European state, which possesses colonies abroad, has a more useful class of subjects than the negroes would be, if they were emancipated in a regular and prudential

tial manner. By degrees they would grow opulent. By their industry as laborers, they would gradually acquire property in countries which afford such a variety of resources, and such an ample field for profitable exertions. Many of them would soon be in a capacity of renting or purchasing plantations. By these means they would rise to a state of opulence, and the posterity of the African slaves would receive a compensation for the evils inflicted on their progenitors.

These personal advantages, however, which relate chiefly to the negroes themselves, will be deemed by many as considerations of inferior importance, in comparison of the great and almost incalculable national advantages which would infallibly accrue to the European countries, from a well-regulated plan of negro emancipation. The negroes, as it has been already observed, making daily advances in opulence and civilization, far from confining themselves to the use of the bare necessaries of life as at present, would, like all others in similar circumstances, soon acquire a taste for articles

cles of conveniency, and from that step
pass on to a relish for those of luxury. This
is the natural progress of civilized society.

The colonies thus constituted and thus
circumstanced, would make a rapid advancement in civilization and opulence, and
prove an inexhaustible source of wealth to
Europe. They would open an ample field
for commercial speculation and adventure.
They would exceedingly augment the consumption of European produce and manufacture, and furnish new incitements to the in-
vention and industry of the old world. With
the increase of wealth and population in the
colonies, the wealth and population of Europe
would be increased in proportion, and her
industry proportionably excited. This is a
necessary and obvious consequence. The
increased population and opulence of the
colonies would cause an increasing demand
for the merchandize of Europe; this would
aggrandize her commerce, and increase her
opulence, and Europe, in her turn, would
have an increasing demand for the productions of her colonies. Thus, the advantages would be reciprocal; the circulation
would

would be brisk, vigorous, uninterrupted, and extensively diffused throughout all the members of the body politic, though widely distant one from another. If the emancipation of the slaves of Hispaniola, Guadaloupe, and the other French islands, had taken place at a peaceful period, and under a regular and firmly-established system of government, instead of being effected just at the eve of a period of anarchy and disorganization, there is hardly any reason to doubt but the island of Hispaniola alone would, in a few years, have been of more value to France, than all the West India islands, taken collectively, are at present to their European possessors.

It must, however, be acknowledged that the disturbances which have taken place in the French settlements, have so far deranged the colonial system, as to render the present moment extremely critical, and perhaps not altogether proper for the extension of freedom to the unfortunate Africans; but of this, and every other measure relative to the subject, the wisdom of parliament is competent to determine. The plan will, undoubtedly,

undoubtedly, one time or other be carried into effect, and, whenever it is accomplished, will be a blessing to mankind, and an honor to human nature.

Another argument, founded on principles of strict justice, may be adduced against the emancipation of the slaves at present in the colonies; and to put a stop to the importation, without emancipating those already in slavery, would only be a partial act of humanity and justice, and make these unhappy wretches feel more sensibly the horrors of their situation. The objection here alluded to is this: the colonists, in the purchase and importation of slaves, have expended large sums of money, of which it would be an act of injustice to rob them, by depriving them of the slaves thus purchased. This argument we must allow to be just and reasonable. No person who has carried on any kind of traffic, not prohibited by existing laws, ought to be deprived of the capital disbursed, without an adequate compensation. This obstacle might, however, be easily removed. None of the nations concerned in this traffic, are

so

so poor as not to be able, without any great exertion, to make this compensation to their colonists. If the inhabitants of all the countries of Europe and America, now concerned in the slave-trade, would consent to deprive themselves of one meal of victuals per week, the savings produced by such an act of abstemiousness, would, in one year, reckoning the value on an average at one shilling per meal, raise a sum sufficient for the liberation of all the negroes in the colonies, if the number be no greater than one million and a half, according to M. L'Abbé Raynal's computation. And what man or woman, who is happy in the enjoyment of liberty, would grudge to contribute by so easy an act of self-denial, to the communication of this greatest of all blessings, to so numerous a portion of his fellow-creatures? Perish, indeed, the glutton who could refuse so small a sacrifice to humanity!

This measure, however, is not necessary, and is only adduced by way of illustration, to shew how easily good might be done, if men were unanimous in well doing. If, however,

however, the expences attending the emancipation of the negroes could be defrayed
by a voluntary subscription in every European country, it would reflect honor upon
human nature; but as this unanimity is not
to be expected, the compensation to the
colonist cannot be made but at the expence
of the state, and this expence could not be
a great national burden in any country of
Europe, or of the united states of America.
As to our own country, the people of the
the united kingdom are rich, benevolent,
and humane. Britons enjoy true rational
liberty in its fullest perfection, and that liberty secured by the most excellent constitution ever devised by human wisdom. Favored by these incomparable blessings themselves, they could not murmur at a trifling
expence, in order to extend them to their
unhappy fellow creatures. The British senate is composed of enlightened men, eminent for political and legislative abilities,
and for the most liberal and extensive humanity. Would it not be easy to make this
compensation, and to defray other incidental
expences by a tax for that purpose, which
could

could neither be heavy, nor of long continuance? If no other difficulty occurred, this might easily be surmounted.

If the slave-trade be diametrically opposite to every sentiment of humanity—if it be repugnant to reason and religion—and, if the expediency and practicability of its abolition appear unquestionable, the contemplative and philosophic mind will naturally make this enquiry—Why is not this odious system long since abolished? or, rather, why was it ever adopted? By what fatal mistake did such good and enlightened men, as the ministers of Ferdinand, and his successor Charles V. and Father B. de las Casas adopt the measure; and through what infatuation was their plan continued by other nations of their own, and other religions? The solution of these problems must be sought in the circumstances of the infant colonies, so very different at that period to what they are at this time. It was necessary to cultivate the plantations, in order to render the colonies advantageous. The natives were unfit for labor; hands were necessary—at this time the case is different.

ferent. There is now in the colonies a great number of negroes accustomed to labor, and these, if their condition was rendered comfortable by the blessing of freedom, would be sufficient for the cultivation of the soil, and there would, in all probability, never more be any scarcity of laborers. Perhaps the great Disposer of all things, who alone knows how to educe good from evil, might, in the mysterious designs of his providence, permit the establishment of negro slavery at that time, as a partial evil productive of general good, in contributing to cultivate and render useful to man extensive districts of the globe, before uncultivated.

Perhaps, also, the same reasons which concurred to introduce the system, might render its continuance for some time necessary. We ought not too hastily to condemn the actions of men with whose motives we are not fully acquainted, and of whose conduct we are not competent to judge. There is not any reason to doubt of the benevolent intentions of the first projectors of the system of negro slavery. To us, us, indeed, it does not appear easy to reconcile with the dictates of humanity or justice, the removal of so heavy a burden from America, by imposing it upon Africa; but they were anxiously desirous of emancipating the distressed Americans from the tyranny of their oppressors, and in the ardor of zeal, for the accomplishment of so benevolent a project, ventured upon the dangerous expedient of doing evil, that good might ensue; an experiment too hazardous to be made by short-sighted mortals, but which, in the management of human affairs, men are often obliged to make.

The first projectors of African slavery, appear to have been placed in this predicament, and consequently their errors have a claim to some excuse. There is not the least doubt but the parliament of Great Britain has long consisted of men of the most benevolent principles, as well as of the most distinguished senatorial abilities; men who both understood the interests of their country, and respected the rights of humanity, and who would long ago have abolished this diabolical traffic, if they had

not

seen the expediency of continuing it. The proper time for its abolition was not come. There must be a favorable concurrence of circumstances, to give efficacy to every measure, and circumstances never appeared so favorable to the abolition of the slave-trade, as at present. The British parliament has, in different sessions, already instituted many wise and humane regulations respecting the importation of slaves, and set a laudable example to other nations. Religious toleration and universal benevolence seem to predominate in Europe more than at any former period. The apprehension, that if Britain should abolish this traffic, other nations would convert the measure to her disadvantage, seems to have no longer any grounds. During the late and present war, Britain has exhibited herself the bulwark of Europe, and has preserved her excellent constitution inviolate amidst the convulsions of nations, and the wreck of governments. Her capital is immense, and her commerce extended beyond the power of any rival to injure. The general aspect of the world seems favorable to the

abolition

abolition of slavery ; and we may venture to
predict, that it will not be long before it be
abolished by all the European nations, and
we may rely on the enlightened humanity
of the British parliament, that it will take a
distinguished part in this great work, whenever it shall, in its wisdom, discover a coin-
cidence of circumstances sufficiently favorable; but of this, as well as of the whole detail
of means to be used---parliamentary wisdom
alone is competent to judge. Private persons
may hazard their opinions, and amuse themselves with their own speculations; but it
would be an unpardonable presumption in
any individual, however great his abilities,
or however extensive his information might
be, to pretend to direct the collective wisdom of the ancient senate of the nation.
Could it, however, be found expedient, I
should be happy to see the abolition of
negro slavery added to the many glories of
his present Majesty's reign ; that history
might transmit to future ages, that the memorable reign of George III. extended the
comforts of liberty to every class of subjects in
the British dominions, and that his crown
                                                          might

might descend with this additional blessing on it to posterity !

And you, who have so long pleaded the cause of suffering humanity, illustrious senators! desist not from the glorious enterprize---redouble your efforts. Divine Providence will, in time, give efficacy to your wisdom and eloquence, by disposing things so as to make the work safe and easy. The task you have taken in hand, will in time be undoubtedly completed, and whether it be your lot to put the finishing hand to it or not, none can rob you of the honour of having undertaken and promoted the most glorious project that ever was conceived by man !

Projects of a complicated nature, and of momentous concern, can seldom be carried into execution but by diligent endeavours, and patient perseverance, amidst innumerable difficulties, and crowds of unforeseen disappointments and delays. Almost every great undertaking is accomplished by the combined and successive efforts of many minds. Alexander had the glory of conquering the Persian empire; but to his father

father, Philip, belongs the honor of having obtained the command of the confederate forces of Greece, and of having organized and disciplined the Macedonian phalanx, to which his son was indebted for his brilliant successes. And Rome, from a collection of about one thousand houses built of mud, and thatched with reeds, in time became the mistress and arbitress of the world, not by a single effort, but by unremitting perseverance. These great exertions began and ended with blood; tyrannic sway was their object; but you, if you accomplish your undertaking, will reach the summit of unblemished fame. Yours will be the glory of having begun and finished a work of everlasting excellence—the joy of many generations and millions, yet unborn, will call you blessed!

If, however, the time for its accomplishment be not yet come, you will at least have the honor of having laid the foundation of a structure of happiness which will undoubtedly one day be erected, and will never fall to decay.

We

We must own, that it cannot but give pleasure to an Englishman, to see that the British government has done more than any other in Europe towards the amelioration of the condition of the unfortunate negroes. This is not, indeed, to be wondered at, since Britain enjoys the happiness of having at once a benevolent and enlightened parliament, a prudent administration, and a patriotic king, whose name will stand in the annals of Europe, distinguished by the glorious titles, of the supporter of freedom, and father of his people.

Nothing, indeed, augurs so favorably for the future abolition of the slave-trade, as the frequent deliberations which have taken place on that subject in the British parliament, for it is evident that every member of that august body would gladly have closed with the proposals of the advocates for the measure, if they had esteemed it safe and practicable. The philanthropy as well as prudence of those members who have opposed the measure is so well known, that no one can doubt but they would readily give their assent, if they could once see a probability

bility of carrying it into effect, without prejudice or danger to the colonies; and indeed
affairs of such weight and magnitude require
a serious consideration, for evils so deeply
rooted are always difficult to eradicate.
Every thing, however, seems to announce
that a time will come when the system of
slavery may with safety be abolished; and
there is no doubt but when circumstances
appear unequivocally favorable, the British
parliament will unanimously carry the abolition into effect; and the well known prudence of that august body, authorizes a
confident assurance that it will be able to
regulate affairs, so as effectually to provide
both for the indemnification of the owners
of slaves, and the safety of the colonies.

I have trespassed long upon the patience
of my friend, but the importance and interesting nature of the subject will sufficiently
apologize for the prolixity of my discussions.
The whole matter is, indeed, so perfectly in
unison with the finer feelings of human
nature, that I am certain this part of my
correspondence will meet with your entire
approbation. When I consider my own
feelings

feelings in writing, I think I am no stranger
to those which my friend experiences in
reading; for, on this subject I am certain
that our hearts beat in perfect harmony.
Situated, indeed, as I am, in a country
where the hideous spectacle of slavery is
constantly exhibited, I could not avoid the
disagreeable view of this degradation of the
human species; and, indeed, how disgusting
soever it may be, no subject is more entitled
to the contemplation of the moral observer.
It is not wholly in the circles of gaiety and
fashion, that we can obtain a complete
knowledge of men and manners; we must
descend through all the different gradations
from the highest to the lowest classes of
society, in order to make accurate observations on the general state of humanity; and
while we delight ourselves in viewing the
palaces of the opulent, we must not disdain
to enter the cottage of the peasant, or the
hut of the slave, but extend our remarks to
all the various situations and modifications
of life.

The melancholy emotions excited in the
breast of my friend, from so long continued
a view

a view of human calamities, will, however, be pleasingly dissipated by the different nature and tendency of my future communications. The languid interval which interrupted my active scene of life is at an end. I am going to make excursions to various parts of this colony, and shall have it in my power to amuse your moments of leisure, by exhibiting a series of observations on places and persons little known in your country. I shall delineate for your contemplation a picture of the manners of men, and modes of life among the farmers in the wilds of southern Africa; and the variety of natural scenery that I shall meet with in my rambles, will add some agreeable shades, and a diversity of coloring. In the course of two or three days I shall set out on my tour into the country. My first visit will be to Constantia, celebrated for its wines, and from thence to various other settlements of the interior; and I shall be careful to observe every thing that I may think worth communicating to my friend, whom, for the present, I must bid adieu.

LET-

LETTER XXIV.

A visit to Constantia, celebrated for its rich wines---Politeness of
the mistress of the mansion---The wine-cellar---The red Constantia wine esteemed the most---Great and Little Constantia
---The wines of both much alike---A rich, sweet wine called
Constantia produced from plantations in the neighbourhood
---Soil and vineyards at Constantia---Description of the mansion, garden, &c.---How to determine here from what quarter
the violent winds blow---Some radical defect in the preparation of the Cape wines---The simple process used in making
them---Their inferiority, &c.

I HAVE not, as I promised you in my
last, been unmindful of paying a visit to
Constantia, so celebrated for its rich wines.
In our way thither we passed several delightful plantations. On our arrival at the
mansion, we were informed that the master
was gone from home, but the lady made
her appearance, and with much civility and
politeness desired us to alight. We were
                                    immediately

immediately shewn into the great hall, which in all Dutch houses is appropriated for the reception of visitors, and the sitting-room of the family. Our errand being readily guessed, we were conducted to the wine-cellar, where the large brass-bound leagers, ranged on each side, bespoke the wealth of the proprietor. Among the few wine-presses to be met with among the colonists, we here observed one; and there was no want of the necessary vessels for containing the delicious fluid while in a state of fermentation. Our conductor presented us with a glass of their best wine, at the same time enumerating their different vintages. The red Constantia is esteemed the most; it may be reckoned a *bonne couche*, but its racy qualities prevent any one from indulging in it to excess. There are Great and Little Constantia; they belong to different proprietors. The wines of both are much alike, and sold at the same rate. Fifty Spanish dollars is what they now demand for a *half aum*, which runs about eight dozen quart bottles.

There

There are plantations in the neighbour-hood that produce a rich, sweet wine, that, when exported to Europe, assumes the name of Constantia. The original plants, we are told, have been brought thither from Persia, but others assert from the banks of the Rhine. It is natural to suppose that many of the neighbouring planters would intro-duce into their grounds plants from this celebrated vineyard;—a few have succeeded tolerably well, but the greatest part have degenerated, or have been, at least, unsuc-cessful in producing a wine equal to that of the original. A great deal must, no doubt, depend upon the nature of the soil into which they are transplanted, as well as in the mode of managing the grapes. At Constantia the soil is excellent, and the vineyards slope gently down the brow of a hill, on an easterly exposure. The grapes are of a very superior quality; they are al-lowed to hang on the vines till they are perfectly ripe, which gives a richness and mellowness to their wines. From whatever cause the superiority of this wine arises, re-

mains

mains a family secret, and is not likely to
be soon divulged.

The mansion-house is surrounded with
stately oaks, and the different vineyards
inclosed with neat, trimmed hedges of the
same. We visited the garden, which was
well-stocked with all kinds of European
fruit-trees, and neglected not to examine
the vineyard. In the management of the
latter there seems to be no material difference from the others in the colony. The
vines are planted in rows of about three feet
asunder. The luxuriant shoots stretch along
the open space between, and they are at no
pains in affording a support to the vine when
bending under its rich burden; perhaps the
violent south-east winds that blow during
the grape season, may be stated as an objection to the plan of raising the vines from the
ground, and erecting hedges of bamboos,
around which the young shoots might en-
twine;—it would certainly be more favorable in keeping their roots free from weeds,
and in promoting a free circulation of air.

In traversing this part of Africa, you have
only to look to the woods that cover the
sloping

sloping sides of the mountain, to determine from what quarter the most violent winds blow;—the strong south-east blasts incline them to the north-west.

In the preparation of the Cape wines there must be some radical defect, as none of them seems to be relished by an European palate;—being drunk in a new state, they are of a heating quality. The process that is observed in making their wines is simple in itself, and proclaims this happy art to be yet in its infancy at the Cape. When a proper quantity of grapes is collected into a large vat, without being stripped from the stalks, sound and unsound, ripe and unripe, are all thrown in together; a slave boy mounts the vessel, and with his bare feet treads among them till the whole is completely mashed and broken. The juice thus expressed is conveyed to the proper vessel ready to receive it; the vinous fermentation is quickly produced, and to its management while in this state, giving it less or more time to ferment, a great deal is said to depend as to the quality of the wine.

It

It has been frequently asked,—why are not the Cape wines equal to those of the southern counties of Europe? Their grapes are allowed to be excellent; but we do not always find that the materials of industry are best wrought in those countries where they are produced. To whatever European power, in the event of peace, the Cape may be ceded, the melioration of their wines ought to claim its principal attention. In its present state it can never be an object of export; were it otherwise, India opens a vast field for its consumption. But it is time to drop the subject; to dwell longer on this intoxicating theme, my pen might betray both wantonness and levity. For the present, then, adieu.

LETTER XXV.

Manners of the planters in the vicinity of the Cape---Their assumed consequence and ostentation---Small cannon on their
plantations to celebrate their births, marriages, &c----Corpu-
lency of the Dutch at the Cape---Causes thereof---The women
of an enormous size---Anecdote of a boor's unwieldy wife---
The toil of reaching the summit of Table Mountain compen-
sated by the delightful prospects it affords---Ice, an inch
thick, upon the pools of water on the surface of it---Kolbin's
monument sought in vain---Description of the mountain.

IN the vicinity of the Cape the manners
of the planters exhibit a different complexion from those in the more distant parts
of the colony. The former are for the most
part in easy and affluent circumstances, and,
surrounded by their slaves, sway with sovereign authority. They assume an air of
consequence in their intercourse with the
more distant settlers, and affect an ostentatious

tious parade, which, though it may exact, cannot insure respect.

As a necessary appendage to their greatness, they are not without small cannon on their respective plantations, for celebrating the anniversary of the births and marriages of the family, or any other particular days of rejoicing.

The unwieldy size of the human body among the Dutch at the Cape has frequently been remarked, and they seem, indeed, not to have lost much, either in point of size or rotundity, by removing from the mother country. The heat of the climate, together with the natural indolence of all ranks, seems favorable to their growth; besides, we may bring into the account their propensity to animal food, which at all meals they devour, particularly the more distant boors, where the grazing of cattle is their principal occupation, and the cultivation of corn little attended to.

The common hour of dinner is between twelve and one o'clock; when this is finished, they indulge themselves in smoking their tobacco, and afterwards take a nap for an hour

hour or two. The supper is generally the heartiest meal, after which they resume their pipe, and then take their repose for the night. From these concomitant causes we need not be much surprised at the several instances of corpulence which are here to be met with,—a thousand *Sir John Falstaffs* may be seen in one day. I have also beheld female figures from the country enveloped in such a mass of flesh, as naturally excites astonishment;—nay, I have been credibly informed, that a boor's wife in the interior had attained to so enormous a size, that she literally could not move her body without assistance. A party of Caffres, during the late disturbances, having attacked the house she was in, a sense of danger impelled her to make an exertion to escape; but unfortunately the door being too small for her unwieldy body, she stuck fast in the attempt, and thus becoming an easy prey, was sacrificed to the fury of the assailants.

Perhaps my friend begins to be of opinion that I have been long enough occupied in gleaning in the immediate neighbourhood of Cape Town, that it is high time that I should

should direct my steps to some distance from this Cape after European manners and follies. For a while, then, allow me your company, while I endeavour to gain the ascent of the celebrated Table Mountain; and let us enjoy together the delightful prospect which is here offered to the lover of sublime and romantic scenery. No day could be more favorable for the attempt; —though about the beginning of July, when heavy rains might naturally be expected, yet the surrounding atmosphere was perfectly serene, and the unclouded top of the mountain seemed to flatter us with an extensive view of the country around. As we proceeded, the ascent became steeper, and the road more uneven. Masses of huge stones, which the descending torrents had swept along in their course, every now and then interrupted our progress. It is only by one particular path, on the side facing the town, that the traveller can proceed with safety. We passed through a cleft, or chasm in the rock, which narrowed as we ascended. The projecting, craggy sides of the overhanging precipice, conveyed to the mind

mingled

mingled impressions of terror and sublimity.
A few halts were unavoidable; for the limbs
soon became wearied from the continued
scrambling over loose stones and brushwood.
At the bottom of the mountain it was rather
warm, but as we advanced the air became
gradually chill, and before we reached the
top, we might, from the coldness of the blast
that issued from the chasm, have fancied
ourselves transported to the regions of the
north. We at length gained the summit,
and were amply repaid for our toil by the
prospect which it afforded. The town below
us, with the neighbouring hills and gardens,
looked like fairy land, and the diminutive
appearance of the ships in the bay, favored
the momentary illusion. When we looked
to the north-east, we were indeed presented
with a wintry scene,—mountains piled on
mountains, receding from the fatigued eye,
and much higher than that on which we
then stood, bounded our horizon. Their
aspiring tops were white with snow, and
proclaimed the reign of winter in all its
rigour.—A cold, piercing wind blew from
the southern ocean, and obliged us to move
about

about briskly to keep ourselves warm. The pools of water on the surface of the mountain had ice upon them;—on one it was not less than an inch in thickness, and the icicles hung from the pendent rocks of an astonishing size for this part of Africa. Such being seldom seen in the neighbourhood of the Cape, we carried along with us a small quantity to town, as a proof of the cold we had experienced on the summit of the mountain. While traversing along, we looked around for Kolben's pretended monument, but were equally unsuccessful with Vaillant in regard to its discovery. Whether any thing of the kind had actually existed, admits of some doubt; but now, however, no vestiges of it remain: indeed, no monument erected by man could long withstand the furious whirlwinds of this stormy region. The surface of the mountain may be termed flat, though in many parts it is broken into inequalities, and intersected with pools of water, diversified in the season with long coarse grass, and a few arid plants. A flock of goats would not be at a loss for excellent pasture, among the crannies of the rocks,

could

could they be rendered secure from the attacks of the hyenas. The increasing coldness of the day prevented us from protracting our stay in those elevated regions. Amply gratified and delighted with the charming prospects we had enjoyed of the neighbouring country, we retraced our steps, and arrived safely at the bottom, not a little fatigued with our journey; so, with my friend's permission, I shall rest for a while, and resume my pen with greater pleasure.

Yours, &c.

LETTER XXVI.

An early journey across the sandy plain on the road to Stellen-
bosch---Hospitably entertained at a neat-looking mansion---
The little family attentions of the African boors---The farm,
though small, exhibited many marks of industry---The climate
more favorable to vegetation than the soil---Occupation of a
little boy---A supply of water necessary in making choice of a
spot for a plantation---Agriculture little understood at the
Cape---Their implements of husbandry wretched---The journey resumed---Approach Stellenbosch---Arrival and entertainment there---Beauties of the place---Though fifteen miles from
sea, excellent fish to be had---Customary mode of inquiring
the distance of one place from another, and the answer---The
manner in which a boor travels by himself on horseback---
The comfort derived from the large spreading oaks---Hospi-
tality of the farmers---The vineyards here extensive and profit-
able---Utility of a traveller understanding the language of the
country he visits---Several families of German origin in all parts
of the colony---Departure from Stellenbosch.

I MUST now solicit my friend's company
a little further from Cape Town, as I wish
to conduct him across the sandy plain on
the road to *Stellenbosch*.

The

The morning sun had not as yet darted his cheering rays on the path we were about to pursue. The face of nature was calm and serene, and hardly yet awake from her slumber, diffused a solemn silence on every side. We directed our course towards the extensive chain of mountains that stretch along from south to north, and terminate the prospect before us. We were here presented with a picture of awful sublimity and cheerless barrenness. As we proceeded, the path we had to follow was formed along undulating ridges of sand. The slow pace of our horses over this sandy tract, together with the sun's rays powerfully reflected from it, prevented our getting forward so speedily as we could have wished. We had not advanced above twelve miles, when, starting as it were suddenly from the plain, a neat looking mansion appeared in full view. Here we halted for the morning, and were hospitably entertained by the family with simple, but wholesome fare. In an instant the cloth was laid, and the table spread out with bread, butter, and eggs; and heaped plates of excellent grapes from their own vineyard.

vineyard. Prepossessed in favor of the hospitality of the African boors, it was with no small degree of pleasure that I here began in my outset, to experience those little family attentions which insensibly win the heart of the traveller.

We accompanied our kind host in going over the cultivated parts of his farm, which, though not extensive, exhibited many pleasing marks of successful industry. He had but lately began to bring it into a state of cultivation, and from the nature of the soil, (being in a manner wholly sand,) it seemed to hold out no great encouragement to the labors of the industrious peasant. It is astonishing in this country what the soils of a sandy nature will produce:—such is the influence of a genial climate, so peculiarly favorable to vegetation. He complained much of the drought of the season, and the parched state of his vineyard and the gardens sufficiently testified it.

I observed a little boy busily employed in the vineyard in cracking a long whip, so as to scare away the little birds that hovered around, and who committed depredations

on

on the vines. They were obliged to tie up
their house-dogs, (of which, by the bye, no
African house is without a tolerable collection) as they sometimes stole unperceived
to the vineyard, and indulged themselves in
plucking a few grapes from the vine.

In making choice of a spot for a plantation, the first thing to be attended to is a
plentiful supply of water, not only for domestic purposes, but for occasionally water-
ing their vineyard and garden. This may
be one of the causes, why so many fertile
spots are to be met with in this country in a
state of nature, while other spots, in the
vicinity of some running stream, though less
fertile, will always determine the choice of
the new settler.

Agriculture, as well as many other arts at
the Cape, is but little understood. Their
implements of husbandry are indeed wretched: you have only to examine their practice within thirty or forty miles of Cape
Town, and then you may form an idea, by
comparison, of what is to be expected in the
more distant parts of the colony. What is
under the immediate eye of government
ought

ought naturally to engage its first care, and the more distant parts ought in good time to be remembered.

After parting with this hospitable family, we continued our course through a succession of sand-hills as before, not a little annoyed with the increasing heat of the day. The chain of mountains confronting us assumed an awful grandeur of appearance. Their bleak and craggy sides presented an uniform scene of dreariness to the wandering eye;—broken into huge masses of infinitely various forms, the tract of the headlong torrent, and all the bold imagery of nature in her sublimest coloring, excited correspondent sentiments in the beholder. We at length reached the top of a gently sloping hill, immediately below which extends a delightful valley, where, at the further end, is the village of *Stellenbosch*. As we proceeded, the tops of the houses peeped from beneath the waving trees. Descending from this height, we soon entered this charming district, diversified with corn-fields and vineyards. On the banks of the river there were a few neat looking houses, the adjoining

adjoining grounds well cultivated, and every one busily employed in preparing for the vintage now approaching.

On our arrival at Stellenbosch we were well entertained at Wolfrom's, a native of Hesse Cassel, who is not ignorant of the art of making his guests pay handsomely for what they receive. This house being crowded, during the summer season, with visitors from the Cape, may with propriety be called the fashionable resort for parties of pleasure. The whole company breakfast and dine together, and the landlord and landlady preside at table. Many repair thither, who are in a bad state of health, to avoid the heat, and violent south-east winds of Cape Town. Here may be procured the finest fruits in the colony; our table groaned under a load of excellent peaches, apricots, and grapes. In Stellenbosch and its environs, the lovers of calm retirement and philosophic ease find numberless charms:—for my part, I could be contented to pass the remainder of my days there, were it not for the *amor patria* which is natural to every breast. Whether it be rich or poor, fertile

or

or barren, still our own native spot fixes our affections, which are felt the stronger the further we are removed from it; added to the endearing ties of friendship contracted in early life, rivetted by time, and the pleasing retrospect of the pleasures they have afforded.

Though Stellenbosch is about fifteen English miles from the sea, we were well provided with excellent Roman fish for table, caught in Gordon's Bay, being an inlet on the south-east side of False Bay. I must observe, that when the traveller inquires the distance of one place from another in the course of his journey, the question is, " How many *hours* is it?" that is, in what time can it be performed at a quick or a moderate pace? The answer is regulated according to the period of time that they themselves are accustomed to travel it. When a boor travels by himself on horseback, he goes at the full gallop, never sparing the little hardy animal that carries him along. He arrives at his friend's house with his horse as wet with perspiration as if he had been plunged over head in water: he tumbles the saddle off,

off, and allows the almost exhausted animal to roll himself in the sand, without giving himself any further trouble about him.

During our stay at Stellenbosch, the heat of the weather prevented our going much abroad, but the large spreading oaks, (that form successive avenues along the streets,) afforded a cool shade from the sun, and an agreeable shelter from the south-east winds. It was with regret I observed, that a few of the finest and largest oaks had been lately cut down. We visited several of the wealthy farmers in the neighbourhood, and met with that hearty welcome and liberality which so peculiarly distinguish them at this moment. I am well aware of the different opinions entertained of this class of men; regardless of such, I give my gleanings from facts, and the testimony of my feelings.

The district of Stellenbosch is noted for its extensive and profitable vineyards. The Steen wine made here is of a superior quality. The different families we visited always presented us with a glass of their best wine: they indulge themselves in something of a stronger nature, and more suited to

their

their palates;—this is what they call a *sopie*, to which, in the course of the day, they have frequently recourse.

A knowledge of the language of the country through which the traveller passes, is always found peculiarly useful. In enjoying this advantage, he associates with the different characters he chances to meet with in the course of his journey, with a degree of profit and pleasure to himself of which he would otherwise be deprived: by this means the latent character is sometimes brought to light, and numberless little anecdotes are learnt, relating to the condition, genius, pursuits, and employments of those with whom he converses.

During the persecuting spirit, and bigoted prejudices of the fifteenth and sixteenth centuries, when many families were forced to fly their native country, and risk the danger of crossing extensive seas, we may readily suppose that the Cape would not be overlooked by those voluntary exiles in making choice of a settlement to which the comparative mildness of the Dutch government, in matters of conscience, might be a powerful

ful recommendation. At this day a number
of families of German origin are to be met
with in all parts of the colony, whose forefathers were among the earliest settlers at
the Cape.

It was with regret that I found the avo-
cations of business required my immediate
return to Cape Town; you must, therefore,
excuse my not paying a visit to the Paarl,
Draeigensteen, and other delightful retreats
in our neighbourhood till another opportunity. I fondly hope, that ere long I shall
again call upon my friend to take a further
peep into the country,—till then, adieu.

LETTER XXVII.

The original inhabitants of the southern extremities of Africa
---The present Hottentots have lost much of their original in-
dependent character---The Hordes no longer compose one
distinct nation; they are scattered about, and more in a state
of slavery than if actual slaves---Wanton cruelty of the Boors
---Description of their persons, male and female---Their dress
---Employment---A Hottentot encampment of men, women,
and children---Their amusements at night---Garrulity of a
Hottentot woman---Of the dissentions in the upper districts of
Graaff Reynet---Heroism of Reinsberg.

ALLOW me to introduce to your notice
the original inhabitants of the southern extremities of Africa. The character and manners of life of the Hottentot have already
been so accurately described and investigated by travellers, that some apology seems
necessary on my part, when I venture upon
the subject. May I not be indulged in
laying before you the little traits of character
I have

I have learnt from personal observation, and the relations of those, whose opportunities and veracity are equally unquestionable?

There can be little doubt that the Hottentots of the present day have lost much of their original independent character, from their connexion and intercourse with Europeans. The powerful engines of brandy and tobacco, which most savages are fond of, being liberally distributed by the first European settlers, gave a fatal blow to their independence as a body, and eventually led to their complete subjugation. In the vicinity of the Cape you no longer meet with hordes, who formerly united together under the command of a chief, and were wont to acknowledge his authority, and follow his standard. They may be said no longer to compose one distinct nation;—they are to be found scattered over the face of the colony, acting in the capacity of drudges or menial servants to the boors;—more dependent, and more in a state of slavery than if actually *slaves*;—exposed to the insolence of power, the severities of oppression, and the caprices of a boorish disposition;—their whole

whole race, in a paroxysm of rage, stigma-
tized with every epithet of reproach;—their
feelings trampled under, and their services
ill requited.

When they can no longer submit to their
hard fortune, and attempt to escape from
those multiplied injuries which have been
heaped upon them, he who calls himself
their lord and master snatches up his gun,
and pursues the runaway. If overtaken in
his flight, he can expect no mercy. The
master pops his gun at him with the same
indifference that he would at a hare or a
partridge. The frequent instances of this
kind that have occurred, set the matter beyond all doubt; and when the Hottentots
become the subject of conversation, a strong
spirit of inveteracy, and secret wishes for their
extirpation may be discovered in the family
against them. No wonder, then, that they
should fly the haunts of savages, and endeavour to regain their liberty and peace.

The figure of the Hottentot is, upon the
whole, not unhandsome; many of them are
tall, with limbs well proportioned, seemingly
calculated for activity, and capable of enduring

during fatigue. When a Hottentot is in motion, he is altogether animation; his pace is so quick, that he seems rather to fly than to walk:—when he runs, his feet are thrown up behind him in such an astonishing manner, that they hardly touch the ground. How unlike himself a few hours before, when, crouching over the fire, or squatted at full length basking himself in the sun!

The eyes of the Hottentots are peculiarly lively and animated, and in many of the females whom I have seen, they bespeak a languishing softness, which, conjoined to a set of fine white teeth, render them suffici-ently attractive. It is only in the more distant parts of the colony that they appear dressed in the primitive simplicity of their country with their sheep-skins. It some-times happens that a few of them, thus dressed, attend the boor's waggon from the interior to Cape Town, to lead the oxen, or be otherwise subservient on the journey;— they are generally poor enslaved beings, carrying evident marks of wretchedness along with them. They frequently part with their sheep-skins in exchange for old blankets,

blankets, or any other coarse wrappers that
may cover their nakedness:—the female
Hottentots in the neighbourhood of the
Cape are generally clad in this manner.

Having lived for some time in the vicinity
of a Hottentot encampment of men, women,
and children, I had there an opportunity of
observing their customs and manners, and
of gleaning some little matter from my occasionally associating and conversing with
them. Invited by the pleasantness of the
weather, I have at times strolled into their
camp, and passed a few hours in being a
spectator of their night scenes of gaiety and
mirth. When all nature is hushed in silence,
it is then that the Hottentots betake themselves to the song and dance, and let me
not be ashamed to acknowledge, that I have,
perhaps, tasted more genuine pleasure amidst
this harmless society, where the cheerful
countenances of all around excited a correspondent cheerfulness to the spectator, than
I could well experience in the splendid circles of the great. At a little distance the
husband was broiling his steak over the fire,
while his wife sat hard by, dandling a young
chubby

chubby Hottentot on her knee, and hum-
ming a tune to keep it quiet;—others were
busily employed in dancing to the music of
the ramky, (as they call it,) and seemed
highly delighted with their exertions. The
most discordant music possesses a magic
power in setting them all in motion. The
young girls are equally sensible of its charms,
—they have a tolerable ear, and when they
sing evince much natural sweetness and harmony. They are at no loss in amusing
themselves with our fashionable reels and
strathspeys. There was one among them,
with a child in her arms, more inclined to
be talkative than the rest; by the bye, you
must know that they all understood the cor-
rupted Dutch that is spoken in the interior,
and the little I was master of I did not fail
to exercise in encouraging the garrulity of
my fair Hottentot. She was employed at
her toilet in bedaubing her cheeks with an
oily composition of charcoal and sheeps-tail
blended together, and appeared by her manner to think that this sooty coloring added
to her charms. Does not the modern fine
lady of our country, while thus plastering
her

her face with rouge, from the same principle of vanity, fancy herself irresistible? I was anxious to know the sentiments she entertained on the subject; besides heightening her charms, she said, she found it peculiarly useful as a preventive against the scorching rays of the sun. She spoke warmly of the cruel treatment that the boors of the interior had manifested towards some of her relations during the late disturbances, when the marked fidelity of many Hottentots was conspicuously displayed. If a wandering, unarmed Hottentot fell into their hands, instant death was the inevitable consequence.

The Hottentots in general seem to entertain a higher idea of the justice of the British character, than of that of the inhabitants of the Cape; they rejoiced when it was in the possession of the English, and were justly apprehensive, in the event of a vicissitude of fortune, that additional severities would be imposed upon them.

During the prevalence of dissention in the upper districts of Graaff Reynet, you are not to suppose that the whole body of boors

boors were in opposition to the British government. A boor, named Reinsberg, deserves to be noted from the part he acted in
the theatre of war. He was one of those
daring adventurous spirits which great occasions only bring to light, and in a period of
general consternation and alarm, give a preponderating influence to whatever party they
espouse. By all he was looked upon as a
staunch friend to the British interest, and
from his connexion and dealings with the
Caffre nation, had become an invaluable
acquisition. I shall here mention a trait of
his heroism and presence of mind, as related
to me by a friend who had been on the spot.
—At a time when a small detachment of
British troops were in danger of being cut to
pieces by a numerous body of Caffres who
unexpectedly came upon them, Reinsberg
was then in the neighbourhood, and had
under his command about forty boors, who,
upon discovering the Caffres, fled in confusion. In this critical moment Reinsberg
followed them, and endeavoured to rally
them to their post. Having succeeded in
collecting them together, he thus forcibly
addressed

addressed his party;—" That while an Englishman remained, he would fight to the last drop of his blood; and that the first among them who should dare to fly, he would shoot dead on the spot." This laconic address had the desired effect, the English were supported, and the Caffres were forced to give way.—Adieu.

LETTER XXVIII.

About three hundred Hottentots regularly disciplined, and instructed in European tactics---Their abilities and allegiance in the service---The Hottentots' natural antipathy to the boors---Partiality to brandy and tobacco---The mode of insuring their fidelity and co-operation, as adopted by the Dutch--The Christian religion favorably received among them---Their docility, industry, &c.---Envy, &c. of the boors---The Hottentot dance--Illicit love, and its baneful effects---Indolence of the women---Characteristic mildness and innocence.

THE British government have hitherto retained in their service a body of about three hundred Hottentots, who have been regularly disciplined and instructed in European tactics. They have been collected together from all parts of the colony, and in the necessary duties and fatigues of the soldier, have been found highly useful. Upon the first alarm of the disturbances in the interior, they were immediately ordered to the
scene

scene of action, under the command of English officers, being well calculated for a service of this nature, not only from their knowledge of the country, but their quickness in marching and supporting its necessary fatigues; though at times they had their friends and relations to contend with, as partizans of the opposite party, yet few or none of them ever betrayed their fidelity, or discovered a disposition to desert.

The Hottentot has a natural antipathy to the boor, and is not at all averse to be employed offensively against him. In an irregular halting warfare he excels, and can find covert and concealment in an apparently open country, where a British soldier would instantly be discovered. Though he is powerfully inclined to inactivity and repose, yet he can be easily roused to exertion. They, indeed, find it their interest to attach themselves to a government that acts towards them with mildness, and supplies them abundantly with the means of subsistence. From the pay that is allowed them they can enjoy their much esteemed luxuries of brandy and tobacco, and after the field-day,

or

or parade, they thus indulge themselves
freely, without any regard of a supply for
to-morrow. To ensure their fidelity and
co-operation, the Hottentot chief, or cap-
tain, must be brought over to your cause,
for still they entertain sentiments of respect
for the head of their horde, though this
respect is at present much abated. On the
first establishment of the colony, the Dutch
did not fail in adopting this political step, to
ensure their allegiance, and soften their
usurpation. When they had conciliated
the friendship of the chief, they acknowledged his authority, and dubbed him a
capitein. As an emblem of peace from
his new master, he received a brass-headed
cane, with the Dutch Company's arms engraved upon it—the price of his liberty and
independence.

Religious sentiments, or superstitious prejudices, are equally strangers to the mind
of the Hottentot. In a state of nature, he
neither knows nor feels that there is a God.
Though possessed of this apathy of character, yet the pure tenets of the Christian religion have been favorably received among
them.

them. The missionaries have been tolerably successful, and formed establishments in different parts of the country. At Bariano-Kloaf, the children are not only taught to read, but the men are instructed in the more useful arts of civilized life; they manufacture knives with considerable ingenuity and address. Thus, the principles of industry are not neglected, together with their religious instruction; and while we teach them to be better, at the same time that we encrease their comforts---every honest heart must rejoice in such laudable endeavours.

The boors of the interior have uniformly acted in opposition to such establishment. They hold in the greatest detestation a poor Hottentot who is without the pale of the church, and pique themselves upon being Christians, yet they would not for the world give countenance to any institution that might tend to the conversion of those poor heathens. They are alarmed at the capacity which the Hottentot discovers for instruction, and fear that, in his progressive improvements, his labours might be more usefully

usefully directed to his own advantage, and
a higher value put upon his services. It is
ever their aim to retain their dominion over
them—to sway them with their accustomed
severity, and to thicken the clouds of ignorance around them. With the savage, as
with the civilized part of mankind, we may
discover an equal fondness for dancing.—
When in the hey-day of youth, we are
more naturally disposed to this expression
of our good humour, and gaiety of spirits;
but how often, my friend, among the polite
circles of civilized society, do the gay and
airy movements of the body, form a striking
contrast to the temper of the mind. When
the savage finds himself inclined to exert
himself in this way, it is following the strong
impulse of a sense of present happiness, and
the motions of his body are in perfect unison
with his feelings. When the Hottentots
are disposed to dance, they are not nice in
the choice of a spot to exhibit in. A small
space is sufficient for this occasion, and they
are in a manner confined to a particular
spot. They hang down their heads, beating
their feet to the music in regular time, while
the

the part behind naturally protrudes, and exhibits a somewhat ludicrous appendage.—Their figure in the dance, is what a *petit maître* would set down as the very antipodes of grace and elegance. As every virtue is mostly accompanied by its kindred vice, thus are the Hottentots by no means strangers to the latter. It is their connection with the European world that has initiated them in meanness, wretchedness, and vice. The dreadful scourge of unlawful love has found its way among them, and, in all probability, has by this time extended its ravages to the utmost confines of the colony. A female Hottentot, a victim to this loathsome disease, and the mean slave of drunkenness, is, indeed, a wretch hardly human, and presents to the reflecting mind, a pitiable picture of European intercourse!

It is a task not unattended with difficulty, to reconcile the female Hottentots to habits of industry. You may often see them formed in circular groups, basking in the sun, literally counting their fingers, as if only destined by Nature to eat and sleep, and while awake to remain in a state of apathy and
listlessness

listlessness. It is only in the moon-light scenes of merriment and dancing, that they become animated, and seem to possess any energy of character. There is a characteristic mildness, innocence, and harmlessness of manner, in the general character of the Hottentots, that but ill accords with those ideas which we annex to a *savage race.*

Adieu.

LETTER XXIX.

A crowd of Malay slaves enjoying the pleasures of a cock-fight---Bets on the match---A new scene of gambling---Reflections on gaming---The slaves at the Cape addicted to this vice---They not only risk their property and clothes, but stake their very children---Often disturbed at their play by the officers of police---Cunning, &c. of several Malay residents in Cape Town, who have obtained their freedom---A Malay priest---The usual employments enjoined by way of penance for sins---The priest acts also as a physician---A Malay funeral---Cursory remarks.

ANY thing novel---any thing out of the beaten track of incident, that I chance to meet with in the course of my perambulations, I find a re-enjoyment of my pleasures in detailing to my friend. There are a thousand little things that to me have their respective charms, but which are perhaps coldly observed, or totally over-looked by others

others. There are many *ears* left behind
by the sickle, which the master of the field
heedlessly passes by—therefore, be it my
province to glean them, and, by their increase, make them valuable.

The pleasantness of the weather invited
me abroad, and I rambled insensibly till I
at last found myself in the middle of a
crowd of Malay slaves, who, having formed
a circle, were enjoying the pleasures of a
cock-fight, and, after the idle part of our
countrymen, had bets depending on the
match. The keen expression of their countenances, and the warm interest of the
spectators, excited my curiosity. I mingled
with the crowd, and could be at no loss to
infer, from the nature of their amusement,
the natural disposition of this class of slaves.
The conflict was obstinate, and the strength
and spirit of the poor animals were totally
exhausted. They are commonly armed
with artificial spurs, and are seldom separated till one of them receives the mortal
blow. The crowd separated into several
lesser circles, and a new scene of gambling
commenced. The dice-box was forthwith
produced

produced, and the young, middle-aged, and old, pressed close upon each other, and staked their several sums. It was no un-amusing sight to observe the various change of features, as their good or bad fortune prevailed. While the eyes of the one glistened with the gains that lay before him, the other looked sullen and dissatisfied from the stakes that he had lost. The noise and warmth of my brown-complexioned gam-blers, increasing apace, I was glad to make my escape, forcibly impressed with a con-viction of the series of ills that a spirit of gambling must inevitably entail, not only on the gamester, but its destructive conse-quences to society at large.

Among this class of slaves at the Cape, a wild gambling spirit is universally predomi-nant, and is carried to such excess, that not only do they cheerfully risk every farthing they possess, but the very cloaths upon their backs; nay, I have been told there have been instances of staking their very chil-dren, a fact so unnatural as hardly to be cre-dited. The officers of police often disturb them in the keenness of their play; and, when

when assembled for this purpose, they have their out-posts to watch their approach, that they may betake themselves in time to their heels.

A number of Malay families, who have obtained their freedom, reside in Cape Town. From fishing, and a low species of traffic, they gain their livelihood, and can successfully exert a spirit of cunning and industry.

On my way home, I met with a Malay priest, on whose face the wrinkles of age had long taken possession. He was employed in superintending a few of his tribe, who were busily engaged in carrying gravel in a basket, which they threw down upon the road, and thus helped to keep it in repair; I understood that such employment is enjoined them by way of penance for their sins. They seem to be the only class of slaves that interest themselves with the performance of religious duties. To their priests they pay great reverence and respect, are implicitly obedient to his commands, and from their contributions he subsists. While I remained with the good old father, I had

I had an opportunity of seeing he was equally skilful in the art of curing the diseases of the body, as well as the soul. A young woman, neatly dressed, with her long hair closely plaited up behind, presented herself before him, and giving him to understand that she was indisposed, asked his advice. With the greatest composure he took a small box from his sack, and striking into its contents a few sparks from the steel, it immediately caught fire, and emitted a somewhat fragrant vapour, with which he bedewed the forehead and temples of the fair supplicant. It had an instantaneous effect, for she took her leave with a look of gratitude and apparent relief from her pain. Happy confidence! that can thus so easily beguile us into health of body and serenity of mind.

My steps were insensibly directed to the " *house appointed for all living.*" I could not help experiencing sensations of a pleasing nature, in viewing the neat manner in which they Malays dress up the graves of their deceased friends, which are surrounded with stone, and covered over with pebbles.
There

There is, indeed, a mournful, melancholy pleasure in decorating the repository of the dead. An egg was placed at the head of one of the tomb-stones, perhaps as an emblem of the purity of the soul. The burial of a Malay is conducted with respect and decorum. The body is ceremoniously carried to the grave, covered with a white shroud, and fancifully strewed with flowers. All the attendants are dressed in their best attire. The Mosambique and Madagascar slaves conduct these matters with indifference, and an entire neglect of all decency and form : they throw the corpse on a bier, and very unconcernedly commit it to the grave.

The temper of my mind concurring with the objects I contemplated, naturally inclined me to be serious. I proceeded along the sea side, and the regular undulating motion of the waves on the beach, heightened the mournful picture, which fancy was busily employed in delineating. How fleeting are sublunary enjoyments! I felt the last word still quivering on my lips, and a responsive sigh gave solemnity to my utterance.

terance. Mark, how proud does that billow rear its head in its approach to the shore— nay, prouder still is that which follows it! The opposing rock has laid low its white crest, and every succeeding one is doomed to the same fate! How many among mankind, have, like thee, been equally high in expectation, and elevated with hope, just at the very moment when some of those accidents that are thickly strewed in the path of life, were about to overwhelm them for ever! In a length of time, unconscious of danger, they rolled smoothly on like thee, O wave!—like thee have they met the opposing rock, and have sunk into inanity!

Adieu.

LETTER XXX.

The colonial laws established on the surrender of the Cape, in
1795---They sanction no partial division of property---The
chief magistrate, or fiscal---His principal emolument---The
court of justice---How composed and conducted---The burgher senate---The wyk-meester acts as constable---The landrest,
or chief magistrate of a district---His assistants called the
veldt cornets---A military post established, as a check upon the
boors, &c.--The commissary, or ecclesiastical court---Hard-
ships and inconveniences attending it---Its evil tendency.

On the surrender of the Cape into the
hands of the English, in September 1795,
the then existing colonial laws were to remain in full force, and an exemption from
all taxes was claimed and granted.

Here the rights of primogeniture, are
not recognised; the younger son has an
equal claim with the elder, and an impartial distribution of property takes place in
the family; the laws of the clergy sanction

no

no partial division, and even should a daughter make choice of a husband, without the consent of her parents, they cannot withhold from her that portion which is her right, when a division of capital takes place, on the death of either parent. One might suppose that the young ladies, naturally of a warm temperament, might, in consequence, enjoy a greater latitude in making choice of a husband.

The chief magistrate at the Cape, is the fiscal: there is a stated salary attached to the office, but his principal emolument arises from fines, which being a power vested in him as discretionary, is so much the more dangerous to the colonists. During the Dutch administration, this appointment was commonly given to a person sent out from the mother country. The present fiscal is an African. The court of justice, being the supreme civil and criminal tribunal, is composed of the most respectable inhabitants. They do not prepare themselves by any regular judicial plan of study, in order to qualify themselves for the station; plain sound sense, correct judgment, and an
intimate

intimate acquaintance with colonial forms
and regulations, are sufficient qualifications.
I wish I could applaud them for their dis-
criminative justice, and impartial decisions,
but I fear, my friend, that this court of
justice, is too often the court of *bribery*—
When any one supposes himself aggrieved,
an appeal lies open to the governor of the
colony.

To the burgher senate more properly belong the immediate concerns and welfare
of the colony. Their meetings, when occasion requires it, are held in the stadt-house,
and they have a president, whose office is
elective. Every street has its respective
wyk-meester, being a respectable house-
holder, to act in cases of alarm as a consta-
ble, to maintain order, and prevent irregularities.

In the country, the chief magistrate is
what they call the *landrest* of the district;
he has commonly within his jurisdiction, a
number of *veldt cornets,* who relieve him
of a great deal of trouble, and perform all
the drudgeries of office. The districts of
Stellenbasch, Swellendam, and Graaf Reynet,

net, have each their *landrests*. The last-
mentioned district is upwards of five hundred miles from the Cape. A military post
has been established in this distant part of
the country, as a check upon the boors,
and a security against the incursions of the
neighbouring Caffres, and *Schelm Hottentots*.

The commissary, or ecclesiastical court
at the Cape, deserves to be noticed, from
its peculiar privileges and dispensations, and
the hardships and inconveniences which the
colonists must submit to, as a necessary consequence. This court possesses the exclu-
sive privilege of granting licences to parties
intending to marry, upon their paying the
douceur of twenty-five rix-dollars. One day
in the week is appointed for issuing the li-
cence and receiving the fee, from such as in-
tend repairing to the altar of Hymen. What
constitutes the peculiar hardship of this ex-
action is, that, as they never allow these important matters to be managed by proxy,
the parties themselves must appear *in pro-
priis personis*, and sometimes travel many
hundred miles for this purpose, and without
conforming

conforming to this preliminary step, no cler-
gyman in any of the more distant districts,
dare celebrate the nuptials. When we cast our
eyes on the map of this far-extended colony,
and consider the distance between the capital
and its utmost boundaries, the peculiar inconveniences and hardships attending a
compliance with this colonial regulation,
must be striking to any one. They are often obliged to submit to toilsome journies in
their covered waggons, before they can be
lawfully wedded to the object of their
choice. It sometimes happens that the
young boor, rather than perform these tedious journies, when his domestic affairs may
incapacitate him from the undertaking, lives
or cohabits with his fair mistress for a length
of time, nor, till he finds a young family
increasing around him, can he prevail upon
himself to visit the ecclesiastical court. Indeed, it frequently happens, that the preg-
nancy of the lady determines his departure.

Whatever might have been the political
views of the Dutch, in enjoining and en-
forcing this oppressive regulation, its inju-
rious

rious consequences are obvious. A check to population—an encouragement to prostitution—and, finally, divesting the marriage ceremony of its sanctity and respect among the distant settlers.

It may, indeed, make them more dependent on the government at the Cape, and a more accurate and correct return of the interior may thereby be obtained with greater facility. But might not the same end be accomplished (not to use a harsher term) by a measure less impolitic and unjust?

You may find fault with the order, style, and subject of my " Gleanings," but I trust their brevity, and the pleasure I experience in pursuing the task you enjoin, will avert all criticism. In the mean time,

Adieu.

LET-

LETTER XXXI.

Further particulars of the ladies of the colony---Their levity,
familiarity, &c.---Education---Peculiarly fond of dancing---
An elegant theatre erected---Indifference of Dutch husbands
---Several of the Cape ladies acquainted with the English
language---A circulating library lately set on foot.

I SHALL here attempt to present you
with a more enlarged picture of the ladies
of the colony. You are already made acquainted that in personal charms, and mere
exterior accomplishments, they are allowed
to excel; but we must now speak of that
better part of them—the mind, natural dispositions, mode of education, and principal
amusements.

The warmth and influence of a genial
climate, contribute not a little to their
gaiety and good-humour, which, in a higher
latitude,

latitude, amidst the society of the more scrupulous, and morose female characters, would immediately be set down as the high road to ruin. Thus, they are naturally led to be more familiar in their intercourse with strangers, but we should not, on this account, give them less credit for correctness and propriety of conduct. What, indeed, must have a wonderful influence on their sentiments and manners, is, their being constantly attended by, and in habits of intimacy with the female slaves (as I observed in a former letter) who openly bestow favors on such as give themselves the trouble of seeking them. They will always find a convenient hour or season to give a wrong bias to their young mistresses' mind, at a period of life when impressions of that nature, conjoined with physical causes, are not unaccompanied with danger. Custom prescribes to them no regular plan of education. Brilliant and fashionable accomplishments are their only aim, while the more homely lessons of domestic œconomy, are mere secondary considerations. Accustomed to be surrounded

rounded with female slaves from their infancy, they no sooner begin to move, than
they find they are not allowed to assist themselves, but have attendants at their call,
over whom they are soon taught, by the
powerful examples they see around them,
of exercising the imperious tones of command; this, by degrees, is confirmed by
habit, and carried with them into active
life, when they become mothers in their
turn.

The young women are peculiarly fond of
dancing, and display both elegance and
grace, when assembled on such occasions.
Previous to the arrival of the English among
them, parties of this kind were more frequent; indeed, they seem to think that we
have too little *penchant* for these amusements, and that we substitute the more
noisy diversion of bets, horse-racing, &c. in
its stead—perhaps there is some truth in the
remark.

We have endeavoured to introduce among
them, a taste for theatrical amusements. An
elegant theatre has been built at a great expence,

pence, and such gentlemen of the garrison as are theatrically inclined, come forward to tread the Cape boards. Our neighbours, however, in New South Wales, are beforehand with us in theatricals; but they have always at their command, a company renowned for their versatile abilities, and adequate to all the shifting scenes of mimic life.

Should the Dutch be again put in possession of the Cape, they will probably convert the *Cape Drury* into *pakhuises* for commercial purposes. We will pass over the little calumnies that are industriously spread abroad respecting the married ladies of the Cape. Jealousy is not the character of a Cape Dutchman. Some are, perhaps, as regardless of the honour of their family, as the smoke they whiff around from their tobacco-pipes; indeed, a pupil of Godwin's school, could not display, on these occasions, a more phylosophic coolness and indifference.

A knowledge of the English language is not among the least acquirements of the fair-

fair-sex at the Cape. Several of them speak it with fluency and correctness of pronunciation. The residence of the English among them, has not much inclined them to a fondness for reading; this is, perhaps, the more fortunate for them. Had they the same partiality for the romantic tales that annually issue from our press, as the gay fashionables of this country, then might we justly apprehend, from the mode of their education, consequences far more subversive of purity of manners, and social happiness.

A society of Dutch gentlemen at the Cape, have lately set on foot a circulating library. It consists of a tolerable selection from the English, French, German, and Dutch writers. A great portion of that time which is wasted in indolence, and amid the fumes of tobacco, may henceforward be more profitably employed in improving the mind, and acquiring a more perfect knowledge of men and manners. And may we not, also, indulge the fond hope, that the native tribes, who inhabit the southern

ern continent of Africa, may soon experience those happy effects that result from this powerful engine of civilization?

" ———— 'Tis a consummation
" Devoutly to be wished."

Yours, &c.

LETTER XXXII.

Fertility of the climate, and indolence of the inhabitants---
‘lavery prejudicial to industry---The corn-farmers, the most
active at the Cape---A habit peculiar to the climate.

WE may, with some degree of confidence advance, that in no other part of the
world, might the comforts and conveniences
of life be more easily or cheaply attained,
than in this part of Africa. Blessed with the
finest climate, and a fertility of soil that hardly
knows any bounds, it holds out an inviting
hand to the exertions of the industrious.
Although Nature has done a great deal, the
inhabitants may be said to have done nothing, for the little exertion that is required
to satisfy the wants of Nature, is left entirely to the slaves. It would be as easy to
direct the streams of the most considerable
rivers

rivers of the country to a different channel, as to rouse the colonist from his uniform indolence of character. It may with justice be said, that the introduction of slaves into the colony, has entailed a series of ill upon it, which are now, perhaps, beyond the power of redress. How pleasing the picture to behold the free man chearfully engaged in the labors of the field; every movement of his body indicates that to him it is a voluntary employment. Mark the slave—his motions are slow; he looks with a dejected countenance on the soil he is obliged to dig; he watches the eye of his master, and when left alone, thinks every moment that is unemployed, comparative happiness.

Among the different classes of men at the Cape, we must allow that the corn-farmer is more inclined to exertion, and less indolent in his habits, from the very nature of his employment. As soon as day-light appears, he starts from his bed, and has recourse to his pipe and *sapje*; this being done, the slaves are set to work at their respective occupations, and the master generally

nerally remains close with them. If the
house is conveniently situated, he marches
up and down before the door, and at the
same time has a watchful eye over them
while at work. A cup of coffee is the common morning beverage. In this manner
he is for the most part employed till dinner-
time, which is precisely at twelve o'clock.
As it is the custom of the country to indulge Nature in a few hours repose after this
meal, the house becomes as still and silent
as at midnight, and woe betide the slaves
if the clapping of the doors, or the barking
of the dogs interrupt the family slumbers.
If a stranger happens to be present, he is
politely asked, if he is inclined to take a
nap? The question seems to us so much out of
season, that we generally answer in the nega-
tive. Sometimes, indeed, at the termination
of a long morning's ride, exposed to the rays
of a scorching sun, we feel somewhat inclined,
after a hearty repast, to follow the fashion
of the house in this particular. After a few
hours repose we get up refreshed, and pro-
secute our journey in the cool of the evening. The influence of climate induces ha-

bits

bits in which the inhabitants of cold countries find no propensity to indulge. Were
we to calculate the time that they actually consume in sleep, perhaps we should
find it less than that consumed by a similar
class in our country. The lady of the family is alike partial to a nap, and, if we believe the whispers of scandal, it is then that
mynheer becomes " high in blood," and
madam " warm—tender—full of wishes."

Adieu.

LETTER XXXIII.

A visit to Hottentot Holland---Hospitably received at a farmer's
---Customs of the inhabitants---Hottentot Holland Kloof---De-
scription of the district---Houses, &c.---Opulence of the far-
mers---The vineyards---Wheat---Bread---Manner of threshing
their corn.

LET me fly from the slanders and little
calumnies of Cape Town—extend my picture of the manners of the country, and
endeavour to give you a faithful delineation
of things as they are,—

" Eye Nature's walks,---shoot folly as it flies,
And catch the manners living as they rise."

We left Cape Town at an early hour,
and directed our course across that heavy,
wearisome, sandy isthmus, which must be
passed before we enter Hottentot Holland.
Corn-fields and vineyards relieve the eye
from

from the dull, inanimate picture of sand and
sterility.

Towards evening we arrived in the district of Hottentot Holland, and were hospitably received, and well treated at a farmer's house of the name of *Morkle*. We
took up our lodging here for a few days, as
we found that every thing around bespoke a
hearty welcome. We here inquire for no
tavern,—a decent looking house determines
our choice, and the civilities of the family
are the inducement of our stay. They are
not all averse from accepting a small gra-
tuity for these kindnesses, but not a few
make a show of declining the acceptance of
money, though, at the same time, they readily fall upon the means of getting rid of
their affected delicacy on these occasions,
by calling the children of the house, both
white and black, to take what is offered by
way of payment. No sooner has the stranger mounted his horse, than the present is
quickly put into the family purse, and appropriated to domestic use. I have more
than once experienced some little polite
contentions of this kind in the course of our
journey,

journey, and always gained my point in the manner above alluded to.

On the south-east side of our habitation an extended chain of elevated mountains of unequal height, stretch along to the north, naked and barren in the utmost latitude of the expression. Winding along, at no great distance, is the Hottentot Holland Kloof, —the pass, which, in a zig-zag direction, carries you across the mountains. In some parts the ascent is tolerably steep. The large bullock-waggons passing along here at once present a picture of danger and sublimity, while the beasts drag the half-suspended waggons across the mountains.

The district of Hottentot Holland is tolerably fertile, and in the higher parts of the valley you ride over a country highly picturesque and beautiful. It is intersected by two rivers, the *Eeste* and *Laurens,* now containing but very little water in their beds. No doubt in the winter months, when the rains pour down in torrents from the mountains, and carry their collected streams to these rivers, they may then assume a more considerable appearance. Instances have

have been known of the traveller being de-
tained for several days on their banks during
these inundations.

The houses are neat and clean, and in
the enjoyment of plenty, they scruple not
to invite those who pass the road to a share.
The farmers are comfortably lodged, and
the general appearance of their houses, with
that of their manner of living, impresses
rather the idea of the gentry of a country
than that of boors. A few have got extensive corn-fields, and large vineyards. The
general want of inclosures in this country,
gives to the most fertile districts an unim-
proved and bare appearance. The corn-
harvest has been this year uncommonly
productive,—thus, to almost a famine succeeds plenty; but many are of opinion that
the corn-farmer in Africa is no less skilled
in hoarding and forestalling, (and its consequent practices,) than the most noted on
your side of the Atlantic. From the increased demand of the produce of the colony
since the arrival of the English, many of
the farmers have risen from narrow circumstances to opulence, and the same may be
said

said of the grazier. Nothing affords a more striking proof of the opulence of all ranks, when contrasted with former times, than the appearance of the female slaves running about the streets of Cape Town. Shoes and stockings were an article of luxury which no slave girl could formerly indulge in; but now they all boast of their fine silk stockings, and fashionable pointed shoes.

The produce of some of the vineyards of the part of the country I am now in, is from seventy to eighty leagers of wine. The wheat of the colony is excellent, of a reddish color, and a large full grain. There is almost in every house good bread to be met with;—they make use of dough which has been longer kept, and has acquired somewhat of a sourish taste, for leaven:—it is an excellent substitute for yeast.

The manner in which they perform the operation of threshing out their corn, may at first sight be condemned, but when we see how effectually it is completed, and the little that is lost in the process, we shall be apt to suspend so hasty a decision. The corn-ricks are generally built close by these circular

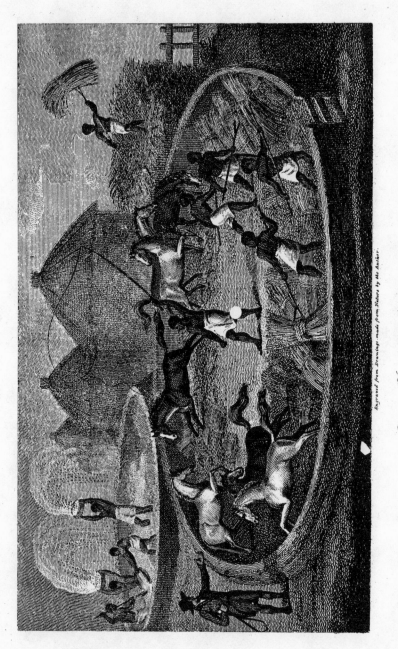

Engraved from Drawing made from Nature by the Author.

The Process of Thrashing.

circular floors, which are surrounded by a fence of clay, perfectly hard, of about three feet in height. When the floor is swept clean, the sheafs are placed upon it, sometimes to the number of a thousand; then all the young horses of the farm are driven round this amphitheatre for a number of hours, till the whole is completely broken under their feet. A person stands with a long whip in the middle of the circle, to regulate their course, to quicken or moderate their pace as he finds it necessary, while a few more hands are employed in turning over the sheafs with forked sticks, so that the whole may have the benefit of an equal pressure. They separate the grain from the chaff by throwing it against the wind, which they continue to do till the lighter part is thus carried away by the force of the breeze. Perhaps a great deal of time and labor might be saved by using fanners, and the grain be more free from sand, of which the Cape flour has always a tolerable portion. —To shake off long established customs and habits in the manners or arts of life, is in all countries a business of time. We are

slow

slow to adopt improvements, though convinced of the necessity of so doing. The
serene, parching atmosphere of the Cape
during the harvest months, hardens the grain
to such a degree, that it does not require
the operation of *kiln-drying* to fit it for the
mill.

In the months of January and February,
when they are most busily employed in
threshing out their corn, and conveying it
to market, they have no rains to dread;—
the violence of the south-east winds may a
little incommode them in their labors, but
no where is this wind so tempestuous and
disagreeable as in town. As the harvest
approaches, and the crops invite the sickle,
the weather becomes more dry and serene;
—with you, my friend, it is quite the reverse,
the moisture of the atmosphere increases
with the yellow tinge of the fields; and the
rains of August but too often overwhelm
the husbandman in ruin. Want of rain is
here the most general complaint; if the
winter months sufficiently soak the ground,
so as to fit it for the reception of the seed,
and a few successive showers bring forward
the

the crop, the husbandman need be under no apprehension of the want of a fine season to gather in the fruits of his labor.

I find peculiar satisfaction in gleaning amid the rural walks of Southern Africa; but I confess I feel at present a diminution of my pleasure, when I reflect—when I see, that the colored group now before me are —slaves.

Adieu.

LETTER XXXIV.

Further particulars of Hottentot Holland---The manner of spending a day---Occupation of a master---Wife and husband---
All is paper currency, instead of specie---Departure from Hottentot Holland---Arrival at Stellenbosch---A visit to Clapmutz, a corn-farm---Polite reception---Striking contrast of
appearances and manners---Of the hay and soil---English
mode of ploughing preferable to that of the Dutch---Invited
to dinner by an old widow lady at an elegant villa---Particu-
lars of her husband---Return to Stellenbosch.

THE pleasantness of the weather, and the
attentions of the family, have induced us to
prolong our stay in *Hottentot Holland.*—
The white, fleecy clouds skim along the
elevated chain of mountains before us, and
portend an approaching south-easter. At the
extremity of the sandy plain, on the right,
the majestic Table Mountain stands insulated and alone, and catches the clouds that
roll along from the southern ocean.

Our

Our house not being more than a few English miles from the sea, we enjoy the cool breeze, and are besides plentifully supplied with excellent fish for our table. We are hardly out of bed in the morning, when the breakfast is announced, and the table laid out with coffee, grapes, and peaches; —the good woman presses us to make a hearty meal, while she herself is occupied in knitting stockings by our side. We commonly amuse ourselves in the interval between this and twelve o'clock, with riding through the pleasant farms in our neighbourhood, and on our return find that dinner is served up,—the table literally groaning under a load of victuals; and a few glasses of country wine wash down our dinner. We then either retire to our rooms, or take a turn round the farm, the good people all this while enjoying their nap. A cup of tea is a common beverage with them in the afternoon; but few, or none of them, think it necessary to add sugar or milk to it. Towards evening the master of the family, and the elder boys, repair to the stable to look after the cattle, and tell over the horses and

oxen

oxen as they are then collected for the night.
Supper is forthwith ready, and that being
the meal which a Dutch boor seems to relish most, he falls to with a tolerably keen
appetite. Less delicate stomachs might be
apt to loath the sight of so much fat, but in
the ideas of the family, the greater the
quantity of greasy sauces, the greater is their
perfection in the art of cookery.

Among the better sort of farmers you
find a person dignified with the name of
Master ;—he is, in fact, the private tutor
to the children, and instructs them to read
and write; besides, he is the politician and
oracle of the family. The woman of the
house reserves to herself the more immediate
management and economy of the family
within doors, while to the husband belongs
the superintendance of the more active labors of the field. The former is seldom
without a large bunch of keys dangling by
her side; thus, in complete armour, she goes
about her domestic concerns,—receives and
pays away money. You seldom meet with
specie in the interior; all is paper currency,
first brought into circulation to relieve a
temporary

temporary distress, but not likely to be discontinued. The English government have extended this visionary fabric of wealth, by the addition of fifty thousand rix-dollars.

After spending here a few pleasant days, we took the road towards Stellenbosch. The general appearance of the country, as we went along, was bare and uncultivated. Beneath the rising hills we met with some neat country houses, and small vineyards adjoining. The running streams from the mountains supply them with water, and where this is to be had in plenty, an encouragement is held out to the labors of the industrious. On our arrival at Stellenbosch, the houses were crowded with parties of pleasure from the garrison at the Cape. Having nothing further to add to my former description of this place, I must beg leave to carry you a little further from the Cape. It is a trite, but yet a true remark, that the farther we remove from the capital, and its immediate vicinity, we are more hospitably and kindly welcomed by the inhabitants. Those nations which we are too apt to call *savage*, generally exhibit in

their

their character and conduct towards strangers more of this virtue, than what is experienced among those people whom we dig-
nify with the title of civilized;—that is, in a
state of society where the genuine feelings
of our nature are kept under, shaped and
fashioned according to the polite notions of
genteel life.

We rode across the country to *Clapmutz*,
situated on the sloping brow of a hill. This
is a corn-farm in the hands of government.
Mr. Ducket, an English farmer, resides here
with his family;—he has been sent out from
home to instruct the boors in the English
method of farming. We were politely received; and the striking contrast of appearances and manners from the houses that we
had just quitted, could not fail of making
impressions favorable to our country. The
Dutch see with surprize large *hay-ricks*,
made from the wild grasses of the country.
The hay being of an excellent quality, and
finely flavoured from the diversity of flowers
and sweet-scented herbs of which it is composed here, having always a warm and bright
sun, it perhaps requires a much nicer attention

Ploughing; with a View of the Governor's Villa near the Cape.

Engraved from Drawings made from Nature by the Author.

tion to the business of hay-making, to prevent its juices from being totally absorbed, than in more temperate climates. This must, therefore, in some measure regulate the process of cutting, spreading, and gathering it up into cocks. From the natural dryness of an African soil, it may be inferred that grass which requires a great deal of moisture, is much less adapted to it than that to which aridity is more congenial. Of the latter kind is the grass known by the name of Burnet, and experiments have frequently been made of its hardy nature. We saw a few of its plants here, which seemed to thrive, notwithstanding the dryness of the season. Green crops of almost every kind are totally neglected in this country, but time and example may effect wonders.

The neighbouring boors view with admiration and astonishment the neat manner in which the English ploughman turns up the hardest soil with only two horses in the yoke, while he, with his large, clumsy, awkward plough, does it in a bungling manner, and requires eight oxen to drive it along. From the continued action of a bright sun,

and

and parching south-east wind, during the summer months, the ground to be ploughed acquires a hard, concreted substance, and is bound together as firm, as if enchained by the hardest frost. The fall of the rains softens the whole, and this is what determines the ploughman to commence his operations. In April and May the rains are looked for, but in the more distant parts of the country they are much earlier. On every side of us, the strong stubble evinces the goodness of the crop, and the fertility of the soil.

Winding along the hill, we arrived at an elegant villa, surrounded with large trees, and vineyards displaying their luscious treasures to the traveller as he passes by. This was the hospitable mansion of an old widow lady of the name of *Melk,* who politely came to the door, and expressed a wish that we should stay for dinner. We were told that she is uncommonly rich. Her husband was a native of Prussia, and came early to the Cape. Being of an adventurous turn of mind, and a judicious calculator, he engaged in colonial speculations, which eventually proved

proved successful; and at his death found himself possessed of a large capital, which our elderly widowed lady now enjoys, with her family, in this charming retreat.

In the evening we returned to Stellenbosch, where I shall leave you for the night, and remain,

Yours, &c.

LETTER XXXV.

Another ride in a northerly direction---The Bang Hoek, a charming romantic spot---A delightful amphitheatre---Its extensive
vineyard, &c.---Departure from it in the evening---Fransche
Hoek---Derivation of its name---The village of Draagenstein
---Arrival at Paarl, a scattered village---The inhabitants
more industrious than elsewhere---Their houses---Hospitality
and good-humor of the hostess---The country altogether a
wine-district---Remarks thereon---Departure from the Paarl---
Arrival at Wagen Maaker Vley---Derivation of its name---Its
fertility---Hospitable entertainment for the night---Character
of the host, who had been a brave soldier---His humanity to a
black child---A visit to Ladikant, a romantic situation.

WITH the prospect of a warm day before
us, we set out from Stellenbosch in the morning, and proceeded in a northerly direction.
—As we ascended the hill, the diversified
scenery on every side appeared highly beautiful;—towards the east the aspiring mountains rose in majestic grandeur, below the
village

village of Stellenbosch, studded with trees, and surrounded with gardens and vineyards; and from beneath the lonely valley pe ped the lowly hut of some hospitable peasant. —In stretching along to the south, a glimpse of False Bay caught the eye. We continued our route in a zig-zag manner along the hill, and were unexpectedly delighted on entering a spot, perhaps the most romantic and charming that this country can boast of;—it is called the *Bang Hoek.*—As we continued ascending, we soon found ourselves in the midst of a delightful amphitheatre, bounded by stupendous mountains, rising almost perpendicular from the bottom, and presenting the sublime and solemn pourtraying of Nature to our admiring eyes. Those enchanting descriptions which are given us of the grand imagery of the scenes of Switzerland, (now, alas! pillaged, plundered, and completely revolutionized,) might even give place to this.—We stayed dinner with the owner of this beautiful retirement, and spent the greatest part of the day in going over the grounds. This vineyard is very extensive;—the whole valley is covered with

groves

groves of orange-trees, and the pigs were running about, feeding upon the peaches and plumbs as they fell from the trees. In favorable seasons, the fruits of the farm probably fetch twelve hundred rix-dollars, and to this we may add eighty or ninety leagers of wine. We observed a few wretched gooseberry bushes in his garden:—they do not thrive at the Cape; indeed, I am ignorant whether the experiment has been fairly tried. This place had something in itself so peculiarly attractive, that it was with regret we quitted it; and having thanked the good people of the farm for the civilities shewn us, we took our leave.—In the evening we rode along the slope of the hill on the west side of the valley, on a tolerable road,— the grandeur of the morning scene was heightened, and the shades of evening gave a parting coloring to the whole, soothing the mind to happy contentment and self-complacency.

On our right lay *Fransche Hoek*, (literally Englished, *The French Corner*,) which appellation it derived from affording an asylum to a few unfortunate exiles of that country,

at

at a period when the mad fury of zealots, and the indiscriminate persecutions of bigotry, had driven them far from home. At this distance of time, both their country and its language have been forgotten. In many parts of the country we met with settlers, whose name and lankness of figure proclaimed them of French descent; while the robust German, and corpulent Dutchman, have preserved their national characteristics in their posterity.

As we proceeded, the valley opened to our view, adorned with more numerous plantations. The village of *Draagenstein* we could hardly discern from amid the surrounding trees. Here some of the best wines of the country are produced, and in this district the labors of the farmer are wholly directed to the cultivation of the vine; for, having a ready market at hand, they soon empty their cellars. We hurried on to *Paarl,* and arrived there late in the evening. This is a scattered village, and extends along the foot of a rising ground. A number of poor tradesmen have resorted hither, where, from the profits of their

their professions, and the advantage of a small spot of ground to furnish supplies to their family, they contrive to live very comfortably. A greater spirit of industry is seen among them, than I have yet discovered in the course of my journey. Their houses are both neat and comfortable, and peculiarly pleasing to him who feels a lively interest in the happiness of his fellow-creatures.

We remained at Paarl for a day, at the house of a good old widow lady, whose gaiety, hospitality, and good-humor, we ought always to remember. We had abundance of excellent fruits. The vintage was on the eve of commencing, which, in all countries, infuses a spirit of gaiety, and at the same time a more ready disposition to oblige. The country I am now in, is altogether a wine district. A great quantity of brandy is likewise distilled from the refuse and stalks of the grapes, and not unfrequently other fruits are added. The Cape brandy is a strong, bad spirit, without any flavour.

From the wine-merchant at the Cape, they were paid about forty rix-dollars for a
leager

leager of wine;—previous to the arrival of
the English, twenty-five dollars was the utmost a leager would fetch. From Paarl,
we crossed the country to the north-east,
and rode through a wild, uncultivated plain,
the surface covered with long heath, which
is the general covering to the parched tracts
of Africa. About sun-set we arrived at the
Wagen Maaker Vley, which, from the near
resemblance of the Dutch word *vley* (a lake)
to our English word *valley*, is generally
Englished *Waggon Maker's Valley*. It has
derived its name from the trees that formerly
grew on the banks of the lake, fit for the
purposes of waggon-building, but now it is
difficult to find out either the one or the
other; it has, however, a variety of trees of
another kind. The most charming orangeries, with their dark green foliage, and the
vineyards winding along the bottom of the
valley, contrasted with the surrounding bleak
mountains, present a picture of fertility and
barrenness highly picturesque. We were
hospitably entertained for the night at the
house of an old German of the name of
Veigh. In the early part of his life he had
                                   been

been a soldier, and in the seven years continental war, participated in the toils and glories of *Frederick the Great*. His manners and appearance bespoke the veteran soldier; and we generally attach an idea of something peculiarly interesting to the conversation of such a character. The name of Frederic imparted a sudden suffusion to his countenance, and he seemed to feel a renovation of his vigor while he acted over again the feats of his youth. The warmth and animation of our *Silesian* hero, gave a double relish to the good things that were brought us for supper. I assure my friend that I never before felt with greater energy and effect the speech of young Norval, in the tragedy of Douglas, in which he acknowledges that he was instructed in the art of war by a lonely hermit; my good old host immediately reminded me of this solitary man,—

> " For he had been a soldier in his youth,
> And fought in many battles."

He has, indeed, made choice of a most delightful retreat to spend the evenings of his

his days;—the groves of orange-trees have
been planted by his own hand; and the
extensive vineyards that wind along the
banks of the mountain stream, have enjoyed alike his fostering care. He is still indefatigable in his exertions, going about from
sun-rise to sun-set in superintending the
labors of his farm.—While at supper, the
goodness of his heart was seen in the treatment of his slaves. A young child was
brought in that had lately lost its mother;
but the kind and endearing assiduities of
the family soon made it forget the loss of
its parent. As the poor little black creature
was about to be sent away, both master and
mistress blessed it with a parting kiss for the
night.—You may think me too minute in
my detail of circumstances as they occur;
but the above you will pardon, from the
more than ordinary impression it made upon
my feelings.—A good bed having been provided, we bade the family good night.

The next morning we visited a most romantic plantation, situated at the head of
the valley;—the road that led to it winded
along the side of the mountain, and we were
suddenly

suddenly gratified with the prospect of luxuriant orangeries and vineyards,—it is named
Ladikant.— It frequently happens in travelling this country, that while seemingly
around all is sand and heath, on getting to
the top of the next eminence, the traveller
is unexpectedly charmed with the sight of
waving trees and luxuriant vegetation.

Yours, &c.

LETTER XXXVI.

Departure from Wagen Maaker Vley—An extensive valley—
Hospitable fare at a poor peasant's—Cursory remarks—Pic-
quet Berg—Vogel Vley ; derivation of the name of this lake—
Rooi Sand Kloof—Lodge at a corn-farmer's ; his surly beha-
viour—The journey resumed early the next morning—The dis-
trict of the Twenty-four Rivers—Stop at a neat looking house
—Kindly entertained—Character of the host—Observations—
The Twenty-four Rivers consist of a few insignificant streams.

AFTER leaving the Wagen Maaker Vley,
we pursued our course to the north, and
rode along the side of the mountain. An
extensive valley opened to our view, vari-
egated with corn-fields. The general appearance of the country is bare and uncultivated ;—the soil naturally good clay,
with a mixture of sand. Having suffered
much from the rays of a scorching sun, we
were glad towards noon to enter the hut of
a poor peasant, who willingly offered us
what

what his house could afford. Our fare, indeed, was neither abundant nor luxurious, but, which made ample amends for both, was given with a cordiality that seemed to tell us we were welcome. It is this, my friend, that enhances the value of the gift, and gives a zest to the most meagre repast. Sheep's-tail was placed before us, instead of butter; the Africans in general relish this disgusting, greasy substance, but our more delicate palates would not allow us to partake of it. As this poor family, were we to judge from appearances, were struggling hard with the world, we took care to pay liberally for what was liberally given. The sight of a few rix-dollars can brighten up the countenance of a boor in his gloomiest moments.

The latter part of the day was delightfully serene. The soil, as we advanced, was seemingly better calculated for agricultural purposes. The mountains on our right increased in height, added to an awful sublimity that irresistibly attracted the wandering eye. Before us, at the utmost boundary of the plain, the towering *Picquet Berg* stood

stood detached and insulated;—there is a romantic wildness in all around:—the feelings strike in perfect unison to the bold coloring of the scene. Stupendous objects impart elevated sentiments, for we are made to feel a lively approximation to the author of our being; the sordid cares of life are dismissed for a while, and the whole heart expands in benevolence and love.

We arrived at *Vogel Vley.* This lake derives its name from the vast numbers of birds of the aquatic tribe that resort thither in the rainy season, and take flight thence when its waters are dried up. The pass of *Rooi Sand Kloof* was upon our right as we proceeded. It winds along the almost perpendicular sides of the ascending mountains, and the bullock-waggons are driven along here in the same manner as at Hottentot Holland. During the dry season, the Rooi Sand Kloof is preferred in travelling into the interior, from the greater certainty in finding springs of water on the journey through the Great Karroo, or desert. Previous to the arrival of the English at the Cape, a journey to the confines of the settle-

ment,

ment, or the *drosdy* of Graaff Reynet, was
considered as a hazardous enterprize; and
it is even acknowledged that the Cape residents were entirely ignorant of those less
distant parts of the colony, which are now
in a manner become familiar to every British officer.   Five or six days are thought
sufficient to perform a journey with relays
of horses, to which the same number of
months might formerly be deemed inadequate.

We made good our lodging at the house
of a corn-farmer on the banks of the Vogel
Vley.   The master of the house was surly
and inhospitable, and endeavoured to incommode us as much as possible, so as to
get rid of us for the night; but as our horses
were fatigued, and the night fast approaching, we thought it more prudent to remain
where we were.   Were we to reckon the
number of his slaves, the extent of his farm,
and the large corn-stacks in his farm-yard,
we might set him down as a rich boor;—
yet, from the absence of every thing comfortable in his house,—from his boisterous
manners,—his unwillingness to please,—and
finally

finally, from his rapacity in exacting the rix-dollars, I may set him down in my journal as a *poor man*. Early next morning we resumed our journey, and directed our course towards the district of the *Twenty-four Rivers*. Here is not so good corn-country as we passed along in the ride of yesterday, —no want of heath, and the soil more sandy. We still kept the chain of mountains to our right. About mid-day we entered the district of the Twenty-four Rivers. A neat-looking house, and every external mark of plenty, naturally induced us to halt. We soon alighted, and were met at the door by the master of the house, whose open, talkative disposition, gave hopes of better fare, and more hospitable treatment, than we had experienced the preceding night. We were not disappointed, but were received with a hearty welcome; and our table was liberally supplied with the good things of the farm. Our host seemed an enterprizing, intelligent boor. He sows about fifty maids (bushels) of corn, and finds his account in making use of manure in his system of farming. In many parts of the country, where a rapid
succession

succession of crops impoverishes the soil, and consequently makes it give but a poor return, a new piece of ground is immediately broken up, and the former cultivated spots allowed to rest till the lapse of a few years restores the principles of fertility. When the farmer is not limited as to his grounds, this is to them a less troublesome mode of procedure than having recourse to those arts of melioration, which in less extensive possessions they would necessarily be obliged to adopt. The new ground about to be brought into cultivation, generally undergoes a few months fallow, exposed to the arid south-east winds, and scorching summer sun, and remains in a hard, concreted state, till the return of the rainy season fits it for the reception of the seed.

We had here an opportunity of remarking a few instances of the industrious exertions of our host. He had, at his own expence, conveyed the water to his house and garden from a stream at the distance of more than three hours' walk. It was carried along the brow of a hill, in a neat, well-formed canal of about four feet broad. He could at will
divert

divert the water thus conveyed to his vineyard and garden, and could likewise flood his pasture ground when it was requisite. Although no rains of any duration had fallen for a series of months past, yet he made no complaint of a scarcity. It was with much pleasure that we traced this canal almost to its source, as a pleasing picture of superior exertion seldom to be met with in this part of the world.

Next morning we rode over part of the district of *Twenty-four Rivers*. We were inclined to explore the streams that issued from the mountains to their source. From the name given to this part of the country, we are naturally led to expect the mighty waters of the Ganges or the Nile rolling beneath our feet; but I can assure you, my friend, that to discover but two or three of those rivers, requires some portion of patience, in riding over heaps of stone and brushwood; and after all this exertion, those *gigantic* rivers dwindle into a few insignificant streams. The larger branch of the *Twenty-four Rivers* issues from a large chasm in the mountain, and a little below it divides into

into various lesser streams. It being now the driest season of the year, we could hardly discover above six small streams issuing from the larger; but no doubt when the torrents tumble from the neighbouring mountains during the wet season, that then the extensive tract before us may be diversified with an endless variety of streams;—but even then they are not to be confined with arithmetical precision to the number of *twenty-four*.

Adieu.

LETTER XXXVII.

The four passes for waggons across the chain of mountains from south to north---Departure from the Twenty-four Rivers---The Great Berg River---Arrive at the neat mansion of an elderly widow---Appearance of the country---Hospitality of the widow---Remarks on the corn-farms of the boors-- Want of waggons to convey the produce to market---Departure from the mansion---The landlady's son offers to be a guide---Swartland ---Arrive at Tea Fontyne---Hospitably received at the mansion of the Slabers.

THERE are only four passes for waggons across the chain of mountains from south to north, into the interior parts of the country, namely—the Hottentot Holland Kloof, Roi Sand Kloof, the Candow, and Pigueners Kloof; the two first are the most common passes. In the afternoon we left the district of the Twenty-four Rivers, and inclining more to the westward, crossed the Great Berg River,

River, the water of which hardly reached the stirrups of our saddles. The vast deep gullies that branch in every direction, shew that in the rainy season it would be impossible to cross this river where we now did. The bed of the river, which we made use of as a road, in a few months hence would certainly bury the traveller who would dare to venture this way, in its overwhelming torrents. The country hereabouts is thinly inhabited. In the evening we arrived at the neat mansion of an elderly widow lady, at the foot of the Reesbech Kasteel. This part of the country assumes a more diversified and mountainous appearance. We had to ascend a regularly sloping bank, before we arrived at the house, and were met by this truly hospitable lady at the door, who, in the genuine accents of a hearty welcome, bid us alight, and partake of the best she could afford—*"Wat wilt gy gebruck?"* (What would you wish to have?) is the first and most common terms of address, on entering a Boor's house. Here this question was put to us, accompanied with a manner and

and a wish to oblige, that set us entirely at our ease.

This is an excellent corn farm; it produces in a good year, fifty waggon loads of corn. One great obstacle to agricultural improvements, is the great distance from Cape Town, and the difficulty and trouble in conveying their produce to market. Their large bullock-waggons are employed for this purpose, and when the weather is hot, they travel during the night, and allow their cattle to be un-yoked, when the sun-beams are powerful. They are then permitted to wander about in search of pasture, under the care of a Hot-tentot boy, and the cracking of the long whip is to them the signal of departure.

In fact, a corn-boor removed some days' journey from town, is afraid to encrease his crop, from the circumstances and expence attending its conveyance to market, and the time consumed in going and returning. The number of maids each waggon con-tains, is generally ten, and we may easily conceive the increased number of waggons it would require, to convey to market an increased produce: eight, ten, twelve, sometimes

times sixteen oxen are allotted to one waggon—each of these specific numbers goes
by the name of a *spann*.

In many parts of the country, large heaps
of straw are allowed to rot, or to be scattered about by the winds, merely from this
circumstance—want of the necessary conveyance for carrying it to town.

To convert the straw to purposes of manure, or apply it as bedding for their cattle,
is alike disregarded by them.

The garden supplied us with excellent
fruits, and we had every inducement to prolong our stay. In the cool of the evening
we parted from this hospitable family, receiving the friendly modes of kissing, and
shaking hands with all, according to the
custom of the country.

To avoid the heat of the day, we had
purposed to travel by night, and as we could
not set out without a guide, the son of our
good-natured landlady obligingly offered
himself to be our conductor.

We kept our course to the westward, and
entered the higher part of Swartland. We
met with few houses on the road we had
taken.

taken. The evening was delightfully cool; the moon just appearing above the horizon, imparted a cheering gleam across the sandy desert. The heavy bullock-waggons had marked out the road for us, so we followed with confidence.

After a long and tiresome journey, we arrived at a late hour, at Tea Fontyne, the residence of the Slabers, which occupies a number of pages in the volumes of a late French writer, whose vivid imagination, heightened by the still more vivid rays of an African sun, gives a coloring to this desert country, the native seat of the sports and graces, as the second Ithaca, to which, in his perplexed moments, he wished to return.

We were received with a frankness and hospitality at the mansion of Slabers, which could not be outdone by the most hospitable African.

I feel myself inclined to go to bed after the fatigues of the journey, but shall resume my pen in the morning, till when,

Adieu.

LETTER XXXVIII.

Character of the old lady at Slaber's---Her advanced age---Description of the house---Probable derivation of the Tea Fontyne---Swartland noted for brackish water---Journey resumed ---Outlines of the scenery in the course of the day's journey--- Meet a flock of ostriches---Description of this bird---Saldanha Bay preferable to Table Bay, in some points---Excellent water at Cape Town---The want of water at Saldanha Bay, a great obstacle to erecting a town there---An excellent spring at Hoeyes Bay---Of an English settler at Saldanha Bay, who had long navigated the seas of the Cape---His discovery of a spring of tolerable good water in his garden---Of the vallies---Comfortable lodging at the post-house---Elevation of the adjoining ground---The signal-post erected by the Dutch government.

WE experienced at Slaber's every mark of hospitality and attention, for which his family has been at all times celebrated. The good old lady of the house, notwithstanding she has reached her eighty-first year (an uncommon age in this part of the world)

world) enjoys a good state of health, and still retains a great portion of the vigour and vivacity of youth. She delights in rambling over the farm on foot, and overlooking the operations of her servants. It has never been my lot, till now, to remark the female character, at so advanced an age, possessing that open, chearful, impressive countenance, united with a placid serenity of mind, that is never discordant with itself, nor with those around them. We may readily allow, that the contented mind bids fairer for a long lease of life, than those numbers of human beings that daily meet the eye, a prey to corroding care, and the alternate paroxysms of caprice and discontent. The house of Slaber is, as it were, built on the middle of a sandy desert: the prospect on either side, affords no charming verdure, nor waving roads, but one bleak dreary perspective, with here and there a speck of arable land to relieve the wandering eye. Water is so invaluable amidst the parched tracks of Africa, that a number of places receive their name from the qualities of the water in the neighbourhood.

neighbourhood. The residence of the Slabers, is named the Tee Fontyn (the Tea
Spring). When the rainy season sets in,
it assumes somewhat the color of tea water,
and might, probably, from this have derived
its present name. You meet with Brak
Fontyn, the Brackish Spring; De Eilinda
Fontyn, from the antelope of that name;
and many other springs in the course of
travelling in the country, indicative of the
particular quality of the water. During
the dry season, Swartland is noted for
brackish water, but neither the people nor
their cattle experience any bad effects from
the use of it. When the inhabitants of
another district is inclined to indulge himself in the playfulness of vulgar wit against
his Swartland neighbour, he commonly says
to him in a taunting manner, *that in Swartland they drink salt water.*

In the manners and habits of vulgar life,
there are numberless intervening shades,
which, though generally unnoticed, the
pen of the gleaner may with propriety contemplate—therefore, be this my excuse, if
                                    I have

I have at times, perhaps, descended into a tiresome minutiæ in the detail of rural life.

From Slaber's we directed our course towards Saldanha Bay—a heavy deep sandy road, like most other roads in this country; the waggon wheels still served us as a guide. A variety of beautiful shrubbery and heath lay on each side; at times, from beneath its covert, the timid gryz-boch bounded before us. A herd of bullocks also appeared grazing on the coarse herbage, under the care of a Hottentot or slave; add to these, two or three solitary houses—such were the outlines of the scenery in the course of the day's journey.

We fell in with a flock of ostriches, of about twenty in number. They were alarmed at our approach, and, in their flight, threw up the sand behind them in an astonishing manner. It being the first time I had seen this noble bird in its natural wildness, I was prompted to pursue them, and satisfy my curiosity in regard to their amazing velocity when pursued on horse-back. The colonists give it the name of the

the struis vogel, the struthia of ornitholo-
logists. This bird is peculiarly gentle in
manners, and it gets over the ground with
such extraordinary speed, that the swiftest
horse can hardly overtake it. We were
told that the Arabians successfully practise
hunting them on horseback. When an
ostrich holds erect his long flexible neck, he
generally measures six feet in length. Their
eggs are thought by some to be good eat-
ing, but we all know that to eat of the ostrich was prohibited in the scripture. From
their frequenting dry and sterile tracts of
country, it has been inferred that they drink
little or no water. The part of the country
where we met with them, indeed, presents a
very strong appearance of want of humi-
dity.

Towards evening we came in sight of
Saldanha Bay, winding along with its va-
riegated islands, which at once forms a secure
and capacious harbour for shipping on the
western coast of Africa.

It was in this bay that commodore John-
son attacked the Dutch fleet, in 1782;
and, which is still fresh in our recollection,

in

in 1796, another ill-fated Dutch squadron was captured by Admiral Elphinstone, now Lord Keith.

By many it has been regretted, that on the first establishment of this settlement, the neighbourhood of this bay was not made choice of for the scite of the town, in preference to Table Bay, where ships are hardly at any season secure, and where delays and inconveniences are often experienced.

The excellence of the water in Cape Town that runs in never-failing streams from the lofty Table Mountain, and its proximity to the bay, were certainly powerful inducements to erecting the capital in its neighbourhood, added to the facility with which the India ships might be supplied with it in their voyages to and from India. Such considerations were certainly objects of the first magnitude to the adventurous Dutch.

An almost insuperable obstacle stands in the way of erecting a town at Saldanha Bay, which is the want of water. Could that be removed, by diverting the stream of

of the Berg river to this purpose, so as to
afford the necessary supplies—then, indeed,
might the fondest hopes of the politician
and speculatist be realised. In regard to a
more central situation for internal supplies,
it certainly claims a pre-eminence to Cape
Town.

When a few miles off Hoeljes Bay, there
is an excellent spring of fresh water, which
is named the Mitte Klep (White Rock) from
its proximity to a mass of rock, of a white
color.

The water we had to drink was extremely
brackish, but the settlers at the bay find no
inconveniency from it, and are perfectly reconciled to its use.

An English settler has made choice of
this retired spot to live in with his family.
He had long navigated the tempestuous seas
of the Cape, as master of a whaler, and
from a spirit of adventure and enterprize,
he fancied this an eligible situation for pro-
secuting the whale fishery, as the winter
months are favorable for killing whales in the
bay. The little spot of ground he has got
under cultivation, yields luxuriant crops of
vegetables,

vegetables, although the soil is chiefly sand.
Were there abundant supplies of water, and
sufficient energy in the inhabitants of the
country, then, indeed, might the surrounding dreary prospect be made to smile with
every useful vegetable for the nutriment of
man and beast. A discovery of some importance in this part of the world, has been
made by this Englishman, in digging his
garden, which is, a spring of tolerable good
water, and free from any brackish taste.

The sheltered vallies that we traversed
in our way to the bay, seemed admirably
calculated for the growth of wood, both
for fuel and other purposes. Many parts
one could hardly be without expressing
some astonishment on viewing. The strong
healthy coloring of the leaves of the shrubbery and underwood, growing from an apparently sandy plain, and at this season very
seldom refreshed by a fertilizing shower,
must excite some surprize.

We crossed the ferry in the morning, and
got safely and comfortably lodged at the
post-house, on the west side of the bay.
What

What we had to eat was good of its kind but, unfortunately for our party, the stock of camty wine was exhausted, and our only beverage was brackish water—bad enough, you will say; yet such is the influence of habit, even in matters of *taste*, that our landlord extolled it as excellent and salutary, although the wry faces we made in getting it down our throats, did not seem to accord with his eulogium in its favor.

The ground on this side of the bay is more elevated, and rises more suddenly. On the summit of the highest hill, the Dutch government had a signal-post erected, for conveying intelligence to the Cape. An old dismounted cannon is still to be seen on the top, which was formerly used as the signal of alarm on the approach of a fleet to the coast. The view from the flag-post is at once commanding and extensive, and the bay below is a beautiful sheet of water; but many years must elapse before the genius, the industry, and exertion of man, can render its lonely bank sufficiently interesting

ₜeresting to the contemplative mind.   Permit me to take you down from this elevated
situation, and at the same time to subscribe
myself

Yours, &c.

LETTER XXXIX.

Return to Slaber's---Proceed to Kleplery---Hart-beests frequent this part of the country---Arrive at Greene Kloof---Much resorted to by sportsmen---Formerly the shooting-lodge of the Dutch governor---The neighbourhood infested by Wolves---The depredations committed by them on the cattle---Produce of Mr. Van Renan's farm---Report of his farm---Koe Berg, Botter Berg, and Tyger Berg, visited---Their fertility in Corn---The corn-farmers obliged to send their cattle to graze on the other side of the mountain---A wax candle made from the berries of a small bush---Customs peculiar to the Dutch---Houses wholly built of clay, very common---The shell-lime which is used, excellent---Return to Cape Town.

WE re-traced our road back to Slaber's, and met with the same hearty welcome as before.

We then directed our course towards Kleplery. The hart-beests frequent this part of the country, but we were not so fortunate

as

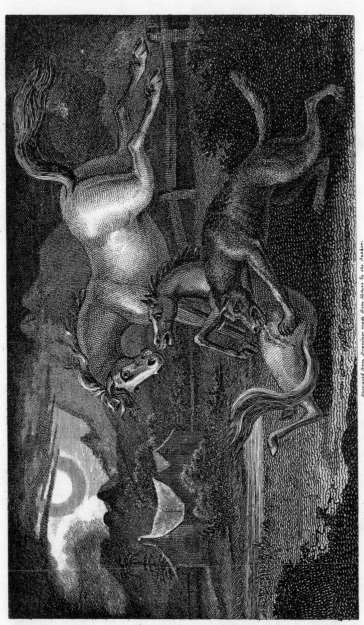

Mare and Foal attacked by a Wolf.

Engraved from Drawings made from Nature by the Author.

as to fall in with any on our road. In the evening we arrived at Greene Kloof. Here is a pleasing variety of hill and dale, and it is much resorted to by the sportsmen of the Cape. This is one of those government farms, which, during the Dutch administration, the governor of the colony always took care to turn to his own emolument and advantage. A tolerably good house had been built here, but it is rapidly falling into decay: every thing around bears strong impression of the ravages of time, and neglect. The Dutch governor and his family were wont to retire thither at certain seasons, and to employ it as a shooting lodge.— Wolves, in great numbers, infest this neighbourhood, and are so bold and daring at times, as to attack their cattle in the kraal, though close by the house. The night before, a young foal had been mangled and torn by one of these destructive animals, in a most shocking manner. The mother of the foal made a noble stand in its defence, but had suffered so much in the conflict, that she died two days after.

A Mr. Van Renan, who has got a large farm

farm a few hours ride from Greene Kloof, carries on his agricultural pursuits with great spirit and enterprise. He is not ashamed to benefit from the example of the English farmer (Mr. Dusket) in the arrangement and management of his land. I shall note down the produce of his farm this year, and the number of his cattle, as related by himself:

1100 muids of barley
400 ditto - wheat
400 ditto - rye
300 ditto - oats
3000 sheep
100 milch cows

A farmer of the name of Pringtloo, is said to possess 18,000 sheep in the distant district of Bruntjes Hoogte. A muid of grain weighs about one hundred and ninety pounds.

On leaving Greene Kloof, we visited the Roe Berg, Botter Berg, and Tyger Berg, small districts in an elevated exposure, and very fertile in corn. From their vicinity to Cape Market, encouragement is held out to them

them for the enlarging their possessions, and encreasing their crops. Their heavy bullock-waggons are almost daily employed at this season, in transporting to the Cape, corn and chaff for the government stores.

The corn-farmers in this part of the country, are obliged to send their cattle to graze on the other side of the mountain, after the labour of their farm is completed, to recruit the strength of their oxen, and put them into good plight. The trifling sum of a few shillings a month, is all that is exacted from them by the grazier, and two or three months at most are sufficient to make them fat.

I observed an excellent kind of wax-candle, at the table of our hospitable landlord, made from the berries of a small bush, that grows in great abundance along the isthmus of the Cape. The process is performed by boiling, and they found it answer better by adding about one half of tallow, to the candles thus made.

The Dutch custom of wearing their hats at all times, and officiously pulling them off in a complimentary manner to strangers, is so well

well known, as scarcely to deserve any notice at this time.   However, there is one
custom, which is peculiarly pleasant if not
healthful, in a warm climate, to which even
the rough and coarse-mannered Dutch of
the interior pay an implicit regard—I mean
the ready attention which is paid to a
stranger in presenting him with water to
wash, at all times; it is never omitted, both
before and after meals. The youngest of
the family are taught to chant a long grace
on these occasions, and I have more than
once caught myself about to fall to, when
the demure countenances of those around
taught me better manners.

Houses wholly built of clay, are very
common among them.   They are sufficiently durable, and their small inclosures
are composed of the same materials. Where
the seasons are only distinguished by wet
and dry, and where, perhaps, from the
month of October, to the beginning of May,
little or no rain falls, this kind of buildings
is found to be perfectly adapted to the
climate. A dry atmosphere hardens the
whole, as if composed of stone. Houses
are

are built with bricks, without submitting them to the power of the furnace, but the influence of a warm sun soon renders them hard. A covering of lime is super-added, and if the weather continues favorable till the whole is completely bound together, then the rain beats against the clay-built mansion without any bad effect. Shell-lime, which is used in the harbour, is excellent of its kind. Saldanha Bay is the grand depot for this useful substance: a manufacture of lime might, to a considerable extent, be erected on the banks of this beautiful bay.

On our return we found, by the violence of the south-east winds, that Cape Town was not far off. We must now, for a few months longer, be annoyed with hurricanes, columns of sand, and every other inconvenience peculiar to this climate.

Having now finished all my intended excursions, of course my Gleanings must terminate. What further novelty I meet with must serve for a personal communication.

If the feeble efforts of my pen have, in any degree, tended to dissipate the gloom

of

of your heavy hours, I shall think the task of friendship, on my side, has been duly performed; if not, it remains for you to act the part of friendship, by accepting the WILL for the DEED, and believing me

Yours, &c.

THE END.